Evelyn Blantyre Simpson

Sir James Y. Simpson

Evelyn Blantyre Simpson

Sir James Y. Simpson

ISBN/EAN: 9783742897930

Manufactured in Europe, USA, Canada, Australia, Japa

Cover: Foto ©Thomas Meinert / pixelio.de

Manufactured and distributed by brebook publishing software (www.brebook.com)

Evelyn Blantyre Simpson

Sir James Y. Simpson

SIR JAMES Y SIMPSON

BY EVE BLANTYRE SIMPSON

FAMOUS SCOTS: SERIES

PUBLISHED BY
OLIPHANT ANDERSON
& FERRIER·EDINBVRGH
AND LONDON

The designs and ornaments of this volume are by Mr. Joseph Brown, and the printing from the press of Messrs. Morrison & Gibb, Edinburgh.

PREFACE

My chief difficulty, in my present effort to limn a portrait of my father that would at once be lifelike, yet as little exaggerated as possible by the unconscious hero-worship of filial affection, has lain in the condensation of the enormous mass of material available for such a biography. What to omit has exercised me more than what to include; while the space at my disposal necessarily precluded any very lengthened dwelling upon specific periods or traits. In this connection, my sincere thanks are due to Mr. Oliphant Smeaton for valuable suggestions, and also for kindly revising the proofs for me.

But such as the biography is, I would lovingly inscribe it to the memory of him who to me was not merely the best of fathers, but the best of men, and whose lessons of love will ever abide with me until I, too, pass to him—'behind the veil, behind the veil.'

EVE BLANTYRE SIMPSON.

EDINBURGH, *October* 1896.

CONTENTS

CHAPTER I
Parentage—Childhood—Schooldays 9

CHAPTER II
Student Days—Start in Life 26

CHAPTER III
The Chair—An Eventful Year—Rise to Success . 36

CHAPTER IV
Chloroform 50

CHAPTER V
Appearance—Popularity—Sympathy 71

CHAPTER VI
Squabbles—Honours 88

CHAPTER VII
Holidays 97

CONTENTS

CHAPTER VIII

ACUPRESSURE—HOSPITALITY—ATTRACTIVENESS . . 106

CHAPTER IX

MONEY MATTERS—RELIGION—TITLE AND AFFLICTION . 117

CHAPTER X

MORE WORK—THE PRINCIPALSHIP—FAILING . . . 132

CHAPTER XI

OVERWORK TELLS—HIS END 147

SIR JAMES YOUNG SIMPSON

CHAPTER I

PARENTAGE—CHILDHOOD—SCHOOL DAYS.

'It is life near the bone where it is sweetest.'—THOREAU.

A MODERN writer says: 'There is to me an inexpressible charm in the lives of the good, brave, learned men whose only objects have been, and are, to alleviate pain and save life'; and as to what constitutes a perfect medical man, a philosopher wrote lately in his journal at Geneva: 'A good doctor should be at once a genius, a saint, and a man of God.' To attain this latter high standard of excellence is a task accomplished by few who, newly graduated, are yearly despatched as 'Argonauts across the rough sea of life, not in search of a shadowy golden fleece, but with a far higher and holier commission; viz. to carry hence the rich and blessed gifts of medicine to all ends of the habitable globe. . . Menecrates wrote true and terse to King Philip of Macedon: "It is your work to kill men; it is my work to save them."'[1] Last century raised up in Jenner a mighty medical warrior, a man 'whose lancet saved far more lives than the sword of Napoleon de-

[1] From *Physicians and Physic*, by Sir J. Y. Simpson.

stroyed.' The medical recruits have a hard but noble career, and noble examples to follow. Wherever there are pain and sickness they find their life's work. Many of them fall battling with the foes of mankind. Some make a big stride onward in their incessant war with death, by finding further means to 'stop his flying dart,' and so gain a niche in the Temple of Fame.

This history is of a 'Famous Scot' who wrought hard to add to the armoury of the disciples of Æsculapius, who never spared himself in his keen pursuit to avert disease, to mitigate pain; one of whom his American medical brethren said, at a meeting held at his death at Washington: 'Prophet, philosopher, worker, and saint, they were gathered together in James Young Simpson.'

This man, who, while seeking to relieve his fellow-men, made for himself a world-wide reputation, was born, 7th June 1811, at Bathgate, Linlithgowshire. His father, David Simpson, was the village baker, so the future physician had to climb up the ladder of fame from a lowly rung. His forebears were of sturdy labouring farmer stock. From them can be traced the source from whence their descendant drew his tastes through the variable trail of heredity. James's grandfather, Alexander Simpson of Slackend, near Torphichen, along with his farming practised farriery, and in the district was much sought after for his skill in the cure of beasts; and this art of healing, which ran in his family, descended in full force on his grandchild. A letter from this sagacious husbandman, dated 1783, still remains in our possession. It is addressed to his sons, and abruptly begins, 'Davied and Gorge.' These lads had journeyed off to London on foot 'to see the world,' for in their young blood ran the desire for a wider view of things than could be got from a small Lowland farm. Their father was anxious about them. 'This coms to let you both know that we are all in some mesure of helth at present, blessed be He who gives it. Your mother has had a long sore troubel, but she is a deall better. Your letters befor was like a cure to her, but your last made her to trembel.' The reason of the mother's fears was the pressgang, which had nearly captured her boys, and neither she nor her husband had any wish for them to serve their country as its defenders. Alexander Simpson had moss-trooper blood in him, for when it was no longer a respectable trade, some progenitor of his, struck by the fatness of the lands of Linlithgowshire, turned his sword into a ploughshare, and settled at Torphichen. The peacefulness of agricultural life had cooled the blood in their veins. The old farmer was no warrior, but he was not lacking in courage. One thing he feared was mad dogs, and to defend himself from one he heard breathing one night in his room, he drew an old sword which hung above his bed. The mad dog on this occasion, on which his wife threw the light of a candle, proved to be a calf that had strayed from the byre, which adjoined the house, and was staggering at the feet of its terrified owner. He preferred that his sons should walk in paths of peace, not 'be soldiers by land or by sea,' as he puts it. He filled the long pages of this letter with much good advice. They had gone forth from their home eager to earn money, but he writes to them: 'Would you desire great riches? It sometimes, when got, takes the wings of the morning and flies away. There are some in our place I have seen great and now verey low; so if you have a small incom and well managed and contentment therewith, you will be as hapey as they that have more.' He ends this long epistle by begging them to keep him informed of their prospects, for their mother 'will be restles till you write. Your letters are not dear, but 10d., so do not spare them; I will gladly pay your fares from whatever port you come, for if your places be not answering to what you expected, come back to us. No more at present, but I rest your affectionet father till death—ALEXANDER SIMSON.'

Alexander Simpson and his wife were an upright, industrious couple, who reared their children well, and along with their daily bread gave them a full share of religious training and the Shorter Catechism. They were people who lived the life Burns so vividly described in the 'Cotter's Saturday Night.'

The elder son remained at home and learned to walk at 'the plough's tail' and work the farm; the younger ones struck out for themselves in whatever line they saw an opening. David Simpson, James's father, being a junior in the family, settled as a distiller at Glenmavis, close to Bathgate. He prospered there in partnership with his brother Thomas, who finally moved to another distillery near Kirkliston. The new excise law, the refusal of the laird of Balbardie, at whose gates Glenmavis lies, to enlarge the premises, followed by the Peninsular war, and the consequent dearness of corn, stopped the distillery. David Simpson next tried brewing, but that did not pay, so he turned his attention to the manufacture of sugar of lead instead of beer. But something went wrong with the compound, and he lost heavily. Having learned baking in his younger days, when he had wandered to London to see the world, he turned to this trade, glad to have some pursuit wherewith to support his wife and some six children that had been born at Glenmavis.

He left the distillery and started anew in Main Street, Bathgate. The Bathgate of these days was very different from what it is now. The click of the weaver's shuttle echoed through its quaint, steep streets, where its inhabitants had gathered closely together for protection in the times when Simsons came a-reiving in Simon Fraser's train up from the Tweed. The Bathgate of to-day has given up roofing with thatch and warm-coloured tiles, and has spread itself out over the flat ground in villas and gardens and rows of miners' houses. The railway is now the highroad and centre of traffic. Main Street, up which the coaches used to pass on their journeys between Edinburgh and Glasgow, is left out of fashion and is falling into disrepair. It remains much the same as it was early in this century, full of quaint houses, mostly gabled and crow-stepped, and with outside stairs. There is a picturesque irregularity about the whole place. The one David Simpson started business in presented a plain face to the street. It could not look straight out on the narrow highway, but was built a little slantwise, leaving room for more cobble-stones on one side of its door than the other.

One piece of good fortune the future Bathgate baker had met with at Glenmavis, for there he wooed and married in 1792 Mary Jervay, daughter of his neighbour, the farmer of Balbardie Mains. This Mary Jervay, on her father's side, was of direct Huguenot extraction. Before the Revocation of the Edict of Nantes, some Gervaises left Guienne and fled for religious liberty to Holland, from whence they sailed to Grangemouth, and settled at Torwood for a while, till they removed to Boghall, close by Bathgate. Here, like the Simpsons, with whom their descendant intermarried, they thriftily tilled their own land from one generation to another. They had allied themselves with those of gentler blood. Mary Jervay's mother (a Mary also) was a Cleland of Auchinlee, connected with the Clelands of Cleland, who in their turn were descended from William Wallace. An American professor, after gazing at Sir James at his own table for some time, exclaimed to a friend, 'I guess your Sir William Wallace had a countenance like Simpson's'; and maybe some drop of the patriot's blood fired his descendant so doggedly to fight the good fight against anguish and disease, that a leading medical paper on his death could say : 'No braver or more brilliant soldier in the army of medicine has in those days been carried to the rear.'

From the Jervays' French extraction many traits in James Simpson's character are traceable. His stubborn defence, whether worldly-wise or no, of what he believed to be right, his nimbleness of thought, his versatility, his sunniness of temper, were doubtless due to some strain inherited from those who had left the gay land of France for 'the dark, the true, the tender North.' The dash of Southern blood which these industrious strangers infused into the deliberate, determined Lowland Scots with whom they intermarried, were qualities which blended with and brightened the somewhat 'dour' Northern stock from which James Simpson sprang.

Such, as far as we know, was the ancestry of the future doctor, and he, like his fellow-professor, Blackie, might truly say: 'I desire to thank God for the good stock-in-trade, so to speak, which I inherited from my parents for the business of life.' There were one daughter and six other sons in the baker's house, in the steep Bathgate street, when the seventh son was born, and James Simpson's mother was no doubt pitied by her neighbours on this addition to her already large family, little dreaming that, when he left this world, the Premier of the land would say (as Mr. Gladstone did on the occasion), in the lobby of the House of Commons: 'Sir James Simpson's death is a grievous loss to the nation; it is truly a national concern.' Bad times had lowered over David Simpson's household before James's arrival in midsummer. Fever had been rife, and some of the elder children were still suffering from it. Money was scarce, sickness and embarrassments had run the household into debt, 'but the lowest ebb is the turn of the tide.' It was certainly a neap ebb in the fortunes of the baker's family on the 7th of June, when the precipitate James arrived before the doctor. The till held less than it had ever done before. His mother, however, found how the knowledge of their unsound financial state had been, with good intentions, withheld from her, how debt was increasing, credit gone, while ruin and starvation were nigh their door. She rose from her bed when her baby was but a few days old, and faced the difficulties with her husband. She was a resourceful woman, and under her vigilant, industrious management their affairs improved, and the tide of fortune began to flow slowly towards them. The neighbours commented on the luck the seventh son had brought, but in this case the good omen was not the happy augured 'lucky' son, but the sensible administrative brain and ever-diligent hands of the mother. As the business flourished, the baker moved from the bare little house in which his younger children were born to a bigger one opposite, which was for years James Simpson's home, a word he pronounced with a very sweet inflection upon it. He grew from a 'toddlin' wee thing,' endowed with a bewitching smile, which from the cradle to the grave won people's hearts, into a stirring boy of a joyous disposition, always eager of purpose, whether at play or lessons. About the time when news of Waterloo was ringing over the country, James's schooldays began. The four-year-old scholar astonished his teacher by his aptitude to learn and his good memory. The endowed academy which made Bathgate a few years later famed for its educational advantages did not then exist James's first school was kept by a man named Henderson, who, owing to his having but one sound limb,—the other being of wood,—was called Timmerleg. James Simpson heretofore had been noted in the village as a broad-made, towsie-headed laddie, with a merry eye and ready laugh. As a youthful scholar he was distinguished by the title of 'the wise wean.' The Bathgate of his day was, as has been said, a weaving, not, as now, a mining village. The weavers were, more than ordinarily is the case, an intelligent class. There were some born naturalists among them, and the baker's bright-faced lad often stood by the loom listening to the 'wabsters' as they discussed some new geological find or classed some botanical specimen. His impressionable brain thus gained a bent towards research, a longing to learn more of these pleasant manuscripts written large on Nature's hills and plains.

Young Simpson was not only well grounded on the benches at school, but his mother was his best teacher, and, as George Herbert says, 'A good mother is worth a hundred schoolmasters.' Therefore between Timmerleg, the weavers, and his home, where the baker's wife was 'The loadstone to all hearts and loadstar to all eyes,' his early training prospered. His mother gave him freely of the treasures of her mind, and her earnestness, her contentment, her firm God-fearing faith, ever lived in his memory.

Ill-health began to overtake the fond mother when her youngest born became a schoolboy. Her elder sons were started in life; her daughter had gone to keep house for one of them who had started in business in Grangemouth. Coming in from school for his forenoon 'piece,' therefore, Jamie usually found his mother alone, her morning's work over, and the dinner simmering on the hob. If he missed her from the shop, he would find her in her room, fervently praying for those whom she felt she would soon be called upon to leave. The little lad at first stood and watched her anxiously, half fearing she was ill, and as he sidled up to her to see if she were weeping, with her face buried in her hands, she, when aware of his presence (for he had ever a firm but soft-footed walk), seeing his distressed expression, would rise and kiss the doubt from off his face, and with a heartsome smile go about her work as one refreshed. It was her youngest son who knew most of her retiring for prayer when the many household duties she executed so well left her leisure—little oases of devotion and rest which she enjoyed in the level desert of daily monotonous tasks.

When it was seen the boy was able so quickly to master his lessons, his family decided James should be their student, and that they would invest their earnings in his education. David Simpson managed the money affairs of his household with a frank liberality which gave all the 'community' a personal interest in the welfare of the till. The cash-box stood open to all. They took what they needed or wanted, unchallenged. They were all frugal, unselfish, industrious, and each conscientiously added what mite lay within their power to refill that general purse. James's mother, like many another in Scotland who had sent their son from a cottage to College, had cherished the hope to be able to give her James a University career. Her elder boys were at work, her younger ones were so far over their school-days that they too would soon be breadwinners, so there was more chance of money to spare for the Benjamin of her flock. Under her heedful direction, business, since the time when James was a baby, had increased, and David Simpson was again a prosperous man. The other members of this love-ruled republic eagerly seconded her wishes. The brothers, without jealousy, willingly worked for her well-beloved Benjamin. 'To wag his pow in a pu'pit' was likely his mother's ideal dream for him, as she patted his ample 'box of brains,' little thinking how many a mother in the future would bless this son for his courageous compassion for suffering women; for, as they said of him at a medical congress in America: 'Coming together from the uttermost parts of the continent, we go hence to homes where his name is everywhere a household word, never to be forgotten so long as the primal curse, from which through God's grace he took the sting, shall lie upon women.'

When James was nine, his mother died. Her death was a sad loss to the household she had presided over with a rule so blithe and tactful. She had, with her wise foresight, trained her only daughter to follow in her ways, so that Mary took up the reins of her government, and directed affairs with the skill inherited from her mother. James at the time was the least affected of any of the family by his parent's death, because of Mary's good guidance and through the carelessness of childhood. 'My second mother,' he wrote of this sister, 'the only mother in later days I knew'; but visions of her who reigned over her children came back in dim glimpses to him ever and anon throughout his life. He never saw any mother looking energetically to the ways of her household, or mending or making a 'bit bairn's frock,' but his eyes glistened with tears, his face lit up with infinite tenderness as he said in that voice of his so instinct with feeling, 'That reminds me of my mother.' She once had taken him on her knee and darned his torn stocking there and then. 'My Jamie,' she said to him, looking with pride at her neatly executed work, 'mind when your mither's awa' that she was a *grand* darner.' He never forgot it. 'I must give a prize to the best darner in Bathgate school,' he said, when he was a famed man. If he had been a school inspector, the first, and maybe not the least important question he would have asked the girls' class would have been, 'Can you darn?' and he would have added proudly, 'My mother could.'

David Simpson, who had been blessed with so able a helpmate, from all we gather, was 'canty, kind, and crouse.' He loved a joke, and he could tell a story well. He was a man who had the faculty of expressing himself efficiently in graphic words. It ran in his blood, as the love of antiquarian research did in that of his many-minded son. When the day's work was over at the baker's, he and his family gathered round the hearth, and Jamie used to place his creepie close to his father, to rest against his knees, or he sat and gazed up at him as he told the attentive listeners, by the flickering firelight, stories of his farmer ancestry, or the legends of the district. David Simpson, though 'pawky' and well informed, was very superstitious, so the doings of warlocks and bogles were among his stock of tales. With the fascination for gruesome horrors inherent in all boys, James often pled to hear yet again from his father's lips how his grandfather at Slackend, whose shrewd and well-expressed letter I have already quoted from, buried a cow alive. When he failed to heal his four-legged patients, he concluded the witches were interfering with him by baffling his remedies, and had to be exorcised. A murrain fell upon the cattle about Torphichen. Alexander Simpson was unable to save them. He decided therefore that to frustrate the malignant devices of the Evil One a cow must be interred alive. And interred it was! David Simpson, who assisted at this barbarous piece of superstition, told James he was for a long time afterwards haunted by the remembrance of the earth heaving after the grave was closed in.

This same superstitious yet pious grandfather also finished his furrows by ploughing in a semi-circle, so as not to let the witches get an even aim at him as he marched after the plough. The flint arrow-heads which the share turned up were proof to him that evil spirits warred with the tillers of the ground. If magpies flew over his fields, he sowed no more that day. He turned his cart back from its marketward journey if a cat or a hare crossed his path. A beggar woman was sent empty-handed from his door, and cursed the house. When he came in for his dinner, he was told of the maledictions, and he straightway dashed off, knife in hand, in pursuit of her, overtook her, and scarred her forehead lengthwise to remove the curse. He regretted that in his haste he had not operated with sufficient efficacy, for some one of his household fell lame shortly afterwards. His brother Thomas, who had retired from his distillery with money, bought a little farm, Gormyre, and set there aside a piece of ground as a species of tithe to the Spirit of Evil, in the hope that the fiend would let the owner enjoy the fruits of the remainder without molesting him. This free gift to Auld Clootie was carefully walled off, but with native longheaded sense the laird of Gormyre gave the most useless piece of his land for this purpose.

Writing anent superstition in 1861, Sir James in an antiquarian paper says: 'In the same district, within twenty miles of Edinburgh, where my grandfather sacrificed a cow to the Spirit of the Murrain, another near relative of mine bought a farm not many years ago.

Among his first acts after taking possession was the enclosing of a small triangular corner of one of the fields within a stone wall. The corner cut off—*which remains to this day in the same state*—was the "Goodman's Croft."'

Another brother of David Simpson's, George, had been engaged in smuggling on the West Coast before he settled down to legitimate trade as a distiller, and his frays (one of a deadly nature) with the revenue men were retold with gusto to his nephew.

Besides these, and many other tales of his superstitious grandfather, James learned also the history of his country, the daring deeds of Bruce and Wallace, and had implanted in him a love of ancient lore and of the incidents of patriotic devotion wherewith his country's annals abound. Even before he could read he had acquired much by hearsay; but once he could decipher a book by himself, he rapidly added to his knowledge, for his insatiable appetite for information was as strong in him as a boy in corduroys, as when he was a doctor in broadcloth. When asked which he had received the most benefit from, the Bible or Shakespeare,—the latter of which he mentioned at his own table he had read through when a very youthful scholar,—he paused in thought before he replied, 'I really cannot say; but I know this, I would have given them both for an Oliver & Boyd's Almanac, for I liked to know facts about everything.' He had a royal memory for legends out of the storied past, or cut and dried realities of everyday life. The few books which came in his way he read in what Thoreau calls a 'true spirit.' His sister Mary was also fond of reading, and the novels and stories she devoured in her spare hours she retailed to the eager, listening James. A very firm bond of love was established between Mary and the young brother, upon whom her mother had charged her to lavish every care. His eldest brother, Alexander, also took a special pride in guiding aright the youngster they all loved because of his peculiar winsomeness. Her 'heart's wish,' her elder son knew, was that her youngest child might not only be a *great* man, but, as Scott said to Lockhart on his deathbed, 'a *good* man.' Sandy did all he could to further her oft-declared wishes, and he never doubted that James would realise them. 'I aye felt he would be great some day,' this leal elder brother said, prideful pleasure lighting up his rugged face as he heard praises showered on the successful doctor.

Though James was studious, he was no laggard at play. He was very popular with his classmates. Though at home petted by all, he remained unspoilt, anxious to take a share in the work of the combined household. He learned his lessons and kept the shop at the same time. Resourceful, as a youngster, he never was at a loss for a tool; the floury counter served instead of a slate. Others boasted they would do successful deeds if they had this or that, but James Simpson could turn what came readiest to hand into the instrument he wanted. He was naturally amiable and good-tempered, always ready to serve a customer, however aggravating the interruption might be to his studious soul. Without a murmur he would run an errand for father or brothers. The 'bonnie callant' was the name he received at the big house of Balbardie, where he was 'first-foot' of a morning with the hot rolls for breakfast.

James Simpson's childhood 'showed the man as morning shows the dawning.' He had, we have seen, for grandfather a man famed for his curing of the beasts of the field, so that the art of healing and keen perception may be said to have descended on his grandson. He also inherited in full, the force of character, the independence, the self-reliance of his father's people. His mother had endowed him with her affectionate and hopeful nature, her singularly sympathetic and pleasing manners, and a sweet-toned voice. When not yet in his teens, he walked to Edinburgh, eighteen miles off, and in a notebook of this first journey he records that at Greyfriars Churchyard, whither he went, he copied an inscription which he described in his journal as 'taken from an old but somewhat elegant tomb,' and, not satisfied, erased that, and wrote, ''Twas taken from an old but elegant tomb. Date 1655.' As a boy, he spent many an hour in the old kirkyard near Bathgate, looking among the rank grass for the graves with the old inscriptions on them, tracing the carvings which time had mossed over, and, doubtless, pondering over the nameless 'martyrs' tomb.' The Pentlands, to the south, rise up like a green wall from out the carse, and the echo of the persecuted Covenanters had drifted across the plain to the roofless chapel and its burial-ground.

It was from his grand-uncle, George Jervay, that he owed this antiquarian bent of mind so early manifested. This uncle of his mother's kept the Brewery Inn at Bathgate, and his suave manners, his interesting conversation, made it a popular howff in his day. A street in Bathgate bears his name. He was a man fond of collecting antique things. His house, and the garden rich in flowers which surrounded his home, were full of old stones, queer local

> 'Auld nick-nackets,
> Rusty airn caps and jinglin' jackets';

so one has not to go far back to find where the busy doctor drew his love for finding curiosities and studying 'the homes of the silent vanished races.' His childish years were an earnest of his future. A happy boyhood it was, in a home replete with love and peace and plenty. School hours and play hours he fully employed, and as he stood among the loaves, awaiting customers, his curly head was ever bent over some book.

But he was barely into his teens when he had to turn from a schoolboy into a University student, and leave the calm shelter of his father's roof with the honest purpose fixed in his mind to repay his people's generosity, and with an indomitable determination to succeed. He went forth into the battle of life, determined, whatever profession he chose, to be at the 'head of his calling.' High as were the hopes centred on him by his people, they did not dream he would attain so high a place that it was written of him forty-five years later: 'No physician in our time—scarcely, indeed, in the whole history of medicine—has left so broad and deep a mark in the annals of physic.'

CHAPTER II

STUDENT DAYS—START IN LIFE

'Look not mournfully into the past, it comes not again. Wisely improve the present, it is thine. Go forth to meet the future without fear and with a manly heart.'
From an old Tomb.

FOURTEEN seemed to be the age when a 'Bathgate callant,' if he were a 'lad o' pairts,' had learned all the parish school could teach. He was then despatched to College. John Reid, afterwards Professor of Anatomy, left Bathgate thus early. He was two years James Simpson's senior, and when he returned after a session at College, his old classmates gathered round him astonished; 'for,' wrote Professor Simpson, 'the rough country schoolboy, who had left us two short months before, had become suddenly changed into a sharpish College student, wearing an actual long-tailed coat, and sporting a small cane.' Every lad in much-worn corduroys thirsted to go, so as to be able to come back and be worshipped in turn by those who sat on the well-rubbed forms. James Simpson strove to follow in Reid's wake, and at fourteen he too was enrolled as a student in the Arts Classes of Edinburgh University. 'Very, very young and very solitary, very poor and almost friendless,' he said forty years after to his fellow-citizens, when receiving the Freedom of the City of Edinburgh from its Lord Provost, Dr. William Chambers, 'I came to settle down in Edinburgh and fight amongst you a hard and uphill battle of life for bread, and name, and fame; and the fact that I stand here before you this day so far testifies that in that arduous struggle I have *won*.'

In the larger sphere of the College the home-bred lad felt at first unfamiliar and discomfited. He found, though dux of his classes at Bathgate, and called 'the young philosopher' among his relatives, he was not able to acquit himself as he had hoped during his first session. 'He was painstaking, but not a specially brilliant scholar; although,' says one who knew him then, 'his class essays contained vigorous thinking, and a grace of style seldom met with in the literary efforts of a boy of fifteen.' At first downcast, the juvenile student was not long discouraged. He set himself at once to rub off his country rust, so as to be quits with his sharper companions. The independence of his race was also strong within him. He knew how his people had economised and wrought to leave a liberal margin for his expenses, what hopes, what love, his home circle had centred in him. Urged by Professor Pillans, who was struck with the boy's rugged but powerful appearance, and had noted his plucky perseverance, he competed for and won the Stuart Bursary of £10 annually, and tenable for three years, which greatly encouraged him. It made him feel he was not eating the bread of idleness, and he tried to limit his expenses to a low figure. Not that the household at Bathgate were unwilling to give him all he needed, but he grudged to take it. James lodged in the same rooms as John Reid and Mr. MacArthur, who had been a master at Bathgate, but was now, like Reid, a medical student. MacArthur urged them on to study without ceasing. They allowed the growing lad but scanty hours of sleep, for constant work had become their second nature, and they sat up late and rose early, burning the candle at both ends in a suicidal manner. When Reid and Simpson were men of consequence, someone speaking to Dr. MacArthur wondered at their rise in life. 'Yes, but *how* they worked!' he exclaimed; and he did not add he led the van, and allowed himself but four hours' sleep.

The bent of his two older companions towards medicine influenced the younger one. He looked at their books, he listened to their talk, he went to opening lectures with them, and he decided that a doctor's career would be his object in life. 'I was then a very young student,' he wrote, 'at the Greek and Humanity Classes in the College, but I was allowed by Dr. Reid to listen to his first demonstrations at home, and sometimes as a special favour I was taken by him of an evening to hear even one of Dr. Knox's lectures.' The trio lodged together in an upper flat in Adam Street. Three shillings a week James paid for his room. He was careful of every penny when his income was £10 a year. Among his absurdly small expenditures, of which he kept a record, there bulks 'a tippet for Mary'! A proud sister she was on receiving this visible token of her brother's thoughtfulness, and a proud brother he while denying himself some necessary to procure it. Mary had suspicions he did not eat enough, and stores of 'hamely fare' came to him by the carrier, who also acted as postman when letters from eighteen miles distant cost 6d. Along with his meal and eggs and oatcakes came well-darned stockings, for she inherited her mother's fingers, and she expended much energy, which to her was a labour of love, in the starching of his few collars and cuffs. Books were the only things he was tempted to be extravagant on. He was more hungry for them than for dinner. 'Finnan haddies, 2d; *Bones of the Leg*, £1, 1s,' he notes. The choice of his literature varied like his tastes and abilities. *Economy of Human Life*, Byron's *Giaour*, Fife's *Anatomy*, *Fortunes of Nigel*, Paley's *Natural Theology*, were some of the earliest inhabitants of his bookshelves. He began his medical studies in 1827, and worked with an originality of thought which, combined with his sleepless diligence, helped him to gain a foremost place. He took notes, as Opie is said to have mixed his colours, 'with brains.'

Queries appear largely through these notes, and he never was satisfied till these interrogation marks were answered. A restlessly inquiring mind and persistent desire to corroborate facts never left him, and was the foundation of much of his knowledge. He never took statements for granted. He made sure they were founded on a firm basis, and he sought till he found that basis. Professor Masson, speaking of my father, said, with graphic brevity, 'He was a man of encyclopædian knowledge. I sat near him at several dinners when I first came to Edinburgh, and it astounded me.'

Amid his medical studies, for an ease to his brain, he sometimes indulged in the 'sad mechanic exercise of verse,' and many sheets of rhyme written in a boyish hand were sent to Bathgate, and still exist. A change of subjects was his only relaxation in his student days, which were one long, uninterrupted course of work. During the vacation he was busily employed also in improving his education and adding to his learning, but he never grudged time to give a help to those at home. He would put down his books and drive the cart with the harvesters' bread out to the fields, when the baking of it kept others busy. He was always on the outlook to help someone, and generally, moreover, found someone who was glad of such a helper. Dr. Dawson (who attended his mother when he was born, and whose note in his book—'Arrived too late'—the doctor often pointed to in after days, to show how this energetic 'Bathgate bairn' was always ahead of everyone) found in the budding medico a gratuitous and clever assistant. James relabelled his bottles in the dispensary, and was always pleased to lend his aid to his earliest friend. When seventeen, he attended his first patient, Dr. Dawson handing the latter over to his sole care, maybe thinking the sufferer was so far spent that a 'prentice hand could do no harm. This patient, however (who proved tough), was a year his doctor's junior, and they were old playmates. He lived to tell the tale to me this year, a hale man of eighty-four. He spoke of his doctor-schoolfellow as of a pleasant-tempered, laughingly inclined lad, cleverer than his companions, yet in every sense one of them. The amiability in his disposition did not arise from inaneness of character, as it sometimes does, for he had enough flavouring of pepper in him to season his sweetness into wholesomeness.

During one of his first sessions as a medical student, his father wrote to him a brief and rather sad letter. 'James,' he says, 'I am now turning old, and wearing awa' like the snaw among the thaw. I have had a weary winter, but will be glad to see you at Bathgate with the spring.—I am yours in heart, DAVID SIMPSON.'

Shortly before James's final examination, his father's health completely broke down, and his youngest son went home, to prove himself not so much a learned doctor as the tenderest of nurses, till that parent's death in 1830. When the old man, who had been a comrade to his children as well as a parent, died, Sandy took his place and kept the home together.

James found in Sandy a second father. As he often said, he was a lucky youth, for when orphaned a sister and a brother became as parents to him. Sandy married in 1832, but he kept a big share of his savings for James, and an ever warm welcome for him beneath his roof. The student feared that the interruption to his studies, and his anxiety over his father's last illness, would interfere with his passing his final examination; but his family had so firm a belief in his powers of combating these difficulties, that they urged him to try what he could do. This he did, and passed his 'final' with honour, being made a Member of the Royal College of Surgeons, Edinburgh, before he was out of his teens.

After this examination, he went over to Fife to visit some little relatives, and the charm of manner possessed by the youthful medico dwelt in the memory of his small kinsfolk from that date.

He never could keep solely in one groove, paying no heed to what lay beyond it. Botany, zoology, geology, all in turn claimed his attention. He always had to be looking about over hedges to glean some enlightenment beyond that which lay in his daily routine. His strong individuality refused to plod on in the beaten highway.

Though thrifty of time, he was never aggressively busy. He did his work without fuss. He would look up from his book during a journey and point out some object of interest; when writing, he kept an open ear for what was going on around, to join in a laugh, or with some 'sabre-cut of Saxon speech' set others laughing, and all the while his pen wrought on.

His extreme youth prevented him taking his diploma at once and becoming M.D.; therefore, after passing his final examination, he went a while to Bathgate, to consider what would be his next step in life.

Unsuccessful in obtaining a surgeonship at Inverkip, a disappointment he felt severely, he resolved to commence practice on his own account.

His brother David having begun business in Stockbridge as a baker, James boarded with him in 1831. He was glad Inverkip had not wanted him, and a ship's surgeonship, which he had also thought would be employment till he was old enough to have the degree he had taken conferred on him, was not at the time procurable. He became assistant to Dr. Gardiner in dispensary work. He returned to College to study at leisure. During the subsequent winter and summer sessions of 1830-31, he said: 'I attended three courses of the very excellent and practical lectures of Dr. Thatcher.' He saw there was scope, and that a likely opening might occur for him in Edinburgh, where he would be able, sooner than in country practice, to repay his brothers for their investment in educating his 'box of brains.' He became assistant to the Professor of Pathology—Dr. Thomson—at £50 a year. The salary was ample for his wants, and this assistantship gave him the opportunity to continue his medical studies out of the classroom, as well as the time to devote to new theories he formed. He would have none of the traditional modes of treatment till he rested assured none better could be devised.

Of Professor Thomson he spoke in later years as one 'to whom I was personally unknown, but to whose advice and guidance I subsequently owed a boundless debt of gratitude. He happened to have allotted to him my graduation thesis. He approved of it, engaged me as his assistant, and hence, in brief, I came to settle down—a citizen of Edinburgh.' It was Professor Thomson who recommended his pupil to take up obstetrics as his special line, and with that quickness of action which never allowed the grass to grow under his feet, Simpson immediately began to study the subject. He brought to bear thereon 'the habit of patient observance and reflection,' which, Dr. Armstrong observed, 'is nothing more than genius in a medical man.' 'Simpson adopted obstetrics when it was the lowest and most ignoble of our medical arts; he has left it a science numbering amongst its professors many of the most distinguished of our modern physicians,' wrote a contemporary of him in 1870.

To perfect his education before he finally settled to practise, his brothers Alexander and John gave him funds for a foreign tour, which he took in company with the present Sir Douglas Maclagan (Professor of Medical Jurisprudence). In the Journal of this trip his many-mindedness comes to the fore. It is full of notes on medicine and queries on divers subjects, to be answered when references come within reach. He first stayed a month in London, where he visited every hospital and met interesting people. His letters to Bathgate are full of information and criticism of all he saw.

When he crossed the Channel, everything was novel, and he noted not only the different treatment in the hospitals abroad, but the scenery, pictures, historic and literary associations, etc. For instance, he says, speaking of the route from Namur to Huy: 'The long dell which we traversed was interesting in a classic point of view. It is the scene of much of the romance of *Quentin Durward.*'

In his three months he acquired a goodly amount of instruction. He went about with wide-open eyes, and it became second nature to mentally note everything and let nothing escape his ken.

On his return to what he calls 'that most sweet of all sweet countries, old Scotland,' he settled down in 1835 in Edinburgh to acquire a practice. He had remarked a few years previously, when he drove his brother David's cart out to Pilton with the bread, that the air was always clear about Stockbridge, and he believed the valley of the Water of Leith about St. Bernard's Well to be very healthy; so much so that he often recommended it to those who could not go South for want of means. He held that there they got all the sun, untainted air, and shelter from the bitter east. It was perhaps too healthy a suburb to start doctoring in, but he nevertheless put up his doorplate at Heriot Row. In 1835 he was elected senior

President of the Royal Medical Society. Of the dissertation he read on that occasion, in a letter to Sandy he says: 'It is 5 A.M. I have been up all night, correcting the last sheets of my paper. I was up all Monday night, and have done with three or four hours' sleep for several others.' His patients, he reports, 'are mostly poor, but still they are patients. I shall not be disheartened, but shall put "a stout heart to a stey brae," if my health be spared me, and I do hope that I may get practice sufficient to keep me respectably after the lapse of some years, but I know years must pass before that.'

There are throughout his letters of this time glimpses of his frugal ways—thanks to John and Sandy for supplies—also plans to make them last as long as possible. Mary sends him boots, as he thinks the Bathgate ones last longest, 'and,' he adds, 'I wear so many.' But he does not approve of the tackets in them—too noisy, though undeniably thrifty. The young doctor from his lodging had many long tramps in these carriageless days, for though he complained of being weary and lame with much walking, he never dreamed of slackening work by leaving some unremunerative patient unattended. He mentions casually that when he returns from a case at three or four of a morning, he just sits down and goes on with his writing, to save time.

In 1836 he obtained a hospital appointment, which added to his experience. He had learned the whole alchemy of professional success, which he said was 'work.' Patients with fees in their hands, hearing good reports of him, came to Heriot Row to seek out this talented young doctor.

CHAPTER III

THE CHAIR—AN EVENTFUL YEAR—RISE TO SUCCESS

'We are sure to get the better of Fortune if we do but grapple with her.'

SENECA.

IN reviewing his year's work on his birthday, 1838, to a cousin who was presently to be more nearly related to him, he says: 'Last winter was a strange blending of working and romping, of study and idleness, of pleasure and pathology, of lecturing and laughing, of investigating the phenomena of diseases and dinner parties, of agues and quadrilles, of insanity and coquetry. I had everything in excess except sleep, and the paucity of it made room for the superfluity of everything else, good, bad, and indifferent.' That was doubtless a fair description of his life in the valley of the Water of Leith—unwearied diligence, studying, and adding to medical literature. He also wrought hard at his practice, with that quickness to perceive and aptness in executing which won him renown. 'The lancet and the pen,' he said, in a letter to this same cousin, 'are my only weapons to win my way, and a willing heart and hand to wield them.'

He became lecturer in obstetric medicine in the Extra-Academical School, and his class was a success.

He had been gifted with that 'arrow for the heart,' a pleasing voice. This, combined with his affluence of speech, made him a popular lecturer, and whether his theme was medicine, archæology, or religion, he held his hearers in thrall. The thoroughness with which he studied his subject, and the way he had of infecting others with the enthusiasm he himself felt, marked him thus early as a born teacher.

After weighing the *pros* and *cons* of the venture, he decided on beginning housekeeping, and became tenant of 1 Dean Terrace. 'The rent is £28 a year,' he explains to Miss Grindlay, 'front door, self-contained, oil-painted and papered, and a comfortable *home*. What a sweet little word that is! One that I have known only in name, but not in essence, for years. The house is perhaps bold; I was frightened after I did it; but I feel I did right. My practice has greatly increased in this neighbourhood, so I could not dream of quitting it. I have drawn £90 since last January, and probably may make out £300 this year. My landlady is very kind to me, but not civil to my patients, and forgetful of messages, so that I am obliged to move.' His brother Sandy, now a thriving baker in Bathgate, advanced him money wherewith to furnish. He was as proud as Mary was of what she called 'his ain hoose.'

Dr. Hamilton, in 1839, resigned the Midwifery Chair. Dr. Simpson, a year or two previously, had said to some ladies he was squiring to the 'capping,' when the students received their degrees: 'Do you see that old gentleman? well, I intend to have his gown.' He promptly set to work to obtain that now ownerless garment. His youth and his bachelorhood were two things thrown in his teeth. He longed for his brother John's prematurely whitened head, to give him at anyrate the appearance of the weight of years. The latter objection he had been wishful for some time to overcome. His superstitious grandfather, Alexander of Slackend, had married a Grindlay from Bo'ness. Coming home from his first tour abroad, the young doctor went to have tea with a Walter Grindlay, a cousin of his own, whose shipping trade had led him to leave Bo'ness for Liverpool. He found Mr. Grindlay had many daughters, and one of them, he said, reminded him of his sister, which meant he wished for nothing better. After this visit to his kindred he had kept up a correspondence with them, and the letters he sent to Jessie Grindlay were treasured in her dressing-case, where they have lain for nearly sixty years.

At this time he wrote to her, stating: 'Within the last few days I have drawn out a formal application for a professorial chair. I have written some fifty or sixty four-page letters, soliciting testimonials from medical friends; but all these were nothing as regards difficulty or importance, when compared with the present little note, for I write to make an application—a formal application—for a wife, and to solicit from you, not a testimonial in your handwriting, but your hand itself.' He received an answer which satisfied him, and the rest of his letters to '*My* Jessie' were all hurriedly written when his day's work, which began before daylight, was over. Two, three, and four A.M. was the only spare time he had for his love-letters. One P.S. outside the envelope is dated 5 P.M.: 'Fell asleep about three, and have wakened so cold; but I must run to catch the post.'

With his love of rigidly declaring the truth, he was anxious his future wife should clearly understand his prospects, and his love-letters, for a man of so much heart, are curiously taken up with money details, what his expenditure must not exceed, the improvements in his house he must make, and that 'frightful load of debt' —it might even be, he said, £500—he owed his brothers Sandy and John, for his education and start in life.

'I canvassed near seventy consecutive hours, and at last I felt so ill I had to apply to my medical friends,' he reports of these exciting times. He had little hopes of gaining the coveted gown at one time, and put it out of his calculations of future income. He received laudatory testimonials from eminent men in the European capitals and from America, for his pen had never been idle, and the pamphlets on medical matters which he sat up to write before his brief bedtime—or when he thought it not worth while to go to rest, as the day was so near—had attracted attention. The closing days of 1839 were beset with difficulties. He had to get over the hindrance of his single state, and arranged to marry at once. His canvassing for his testimonials (of many thick pages, which he sowed broadcast) had run him still more heavily into debt. The sister so dear to him was sailing with her husband for Australia, and his heart was wrung to think he would not see her again.

His marriage took place on the day after Christmas 1839, and he had to journey back to Edinburgh for a honeymoon trip, as he had to lecture on the 30th. Though his enemies sternly opposed his appointment to the Chair, and made a hard fight against him, he won the wished-for gown when ''40' was still in its early weeks, and at twenty-nine he became a professor. He wrote to Mrs. Grindlay as follows:—'MY DEAREST MOTHER,—Jessie's honeymoon and mine begins to-morrow. I was elected Professor to-day by a majority of one. Hurrah!—Your ever affectionate son, J. Y. SIMPSON.—4th February.'

It is curious, looking back from our vantage of time, to find that one strong objection urged against the junior candidate was that the trade of the town would fall off if one so wanting in influence, and hitherto so unknown, obtained it. The prevision of the Town Councillors who voted against him on that score, could not be expected to see, in a not very distant future, lodgings and hotels thronged with his patients, and from 'a' the airts the wind can blaw' people pitching their camp in Edinburgh to be near his healing skill.

Basking in sunny shallows was not ordained to be Simpson's lot. He was seldom out of some big war or some skirmish, for he was ever in the thick of the battle of life. He never bore ill-will against his antagonists personally, which was hard for them to understand. He fought vigorously for what he believed to be the truth, for the advancement of medicine or the betterment of human kind, not against his opponents as men. Professor Simpson was a man who preferred peace, yet withal was pre-eminently a fighting man. But he always had his temper under control.

Once, however, early in his career, a hasty statement led him to the verge of a duel. At the College of Physicians he called an anonymous letter in a medical paper 'a scandalous, lying article,' and addressed this remark to the writer of it, not aware that he had penned it. Serious results arose from these words. A duel was arranged, though my father had never handled sword or pistol in his life. Some other physicians interfered, however, and the would-be duellists were brought together, and afterwards became firm friends. He had, it is said, no acquaintances, for such was his power of pleasing, so charming his conversation and manner, that high and low who had spoken to him claimed him ever after as a friend.

Neither did fate ever allow him to enjoy the 'sweet serenity' of reading in 'sequestered nooks.' He had to devour books as he drove on his rounds, as he travelled, or as he sat by sick-beds. 'Mrs. Proudie's dead—I wonder if the Bishop is sorry,' he said to a friend, as he went up the steps of her house with Trollope's *Chronicle* in his hand. 'How do you get time to know all the novels of the day?' asked a patient in wonderment. 'By never wasting an "orra moment,"' he replied in the Scots tongue; and not only novels, but through every class of literature he read. He told an old fellow-student it was his habit to keep any subject that might be 'on the stocks' constantly in his mind's eye, and to employ for thinking it out, reading it up, or committing his ideas to writing, the smallest odds and ends of time left vacant in the midst of his daily or nightly labours.

'The goods of life of a medical man wherewith to barter for a living,' he said, 'were his professional knowledge and his time.' He urged upon his students to enlarge the quantity and enrich the quality of the former, and begged of them to save and economise the latter.

His archæological works and his medical treatises prove he practised the precept he taught. He hoarded up all the information he came by out of the printed pages he scanned, and turned it to use when occasion arose. The notes to his antiquarian works, rich in erudition, stored with detail, are full of antiquarian lore. They alone would have been enough to keep a dilettante busy unearthing and verifying, but the Professor had a knack of finding what he wanted. His manuscript notes, written while travelling or by sick-beds, look chaotic, but he sorted them when they were wanted to clinch an argument or suggest a theory. He could disinter from a library the very book which bore on the subject he had in hand. He would get on the track of some ancient writer, and never be at peace till he had resurrected him from some shelf thick with the dust of ages. A librarian said to a savant: 'Professor Simpson comes here for books which nobody but himself, I believe, knows to exist. I wonder how he has time to find out about them.'

When he had his mind set on studying anything, he grudged no amount of persistent painstaking to master the subject. 'When he set himself to think out a subject, all that had ever been written on it seemed to come at once within reach. The mass in his hand became plastic and yielded to his touch, and the heat and radiance of his genius penetrated it,' wrote one who knew him. His devious range of reading 'at orra moments' had tutored him to talk with ease and appositeness to all sorts of people, and kept him ever in the van of thought, from the newest novel, or some antiquarian puzzle, to some bright light made to shine on medicine. Mary wrote to him at this time: 'Every visitor from Edinburgh brings us word of your prosperity, or rather of your industry and its reward;' and she was right. It was pure hard work which advanced him. The genius with which he was endowed he did not depend on.

He never forgot his native town and the friends of his youth. However busy the overwrought doctor was, an 'open sesame' to his time were the words, 'an old friend from Bathgate.' He would willingly toil up the longest flight of stairs in an Old Town 'land,' leaving a duchess on the first floor of a Princes Street hotel impatiently chafing at the delay, to see someone who claimed to be from his native village. The *Daily Scotsman* in 1855 gives an account of how difficult it was often to gain an audience with the Professor. They took it from a letter of Mr. Horace Greeley: 'Go when you will to his house in his "hours," and you will find forty or fifty persons waiting his arrival. Odd stories are told of the number and patience of the pilgrims who early and late besiege the famous oracle; of the importunity of great titles, the sturdiness of unyielding janitors, and the honest Scotch pride of high and low in the popularity of their celebrated countryman. A good-natured authoress relates with gusto, that, taking a sick friend for the doctor's advice, she was informed by the servant that no more patients could be seen that day. "But," said the authoress, "I am sure I can be admitted; take my name, he knows me." "Dr. Simpson knows the Queen, ma'am," was the cool rejoinder, with which the door closed on the disconcerted ladies.'

1840 was a very memorable year for the young doctor. The contest for the professorship had raised up enemies who harassed him throughout his career. It had also left him deeply involved; for to canvass and print and distribute his testimonials—a book, the first part alone of which numbered 134 pages—had cost him some £300. Money owed to Sandy was due. His brother had been meeting other embarrassments, and had need of it. 'Sandy,' he wrote at this time, 'in my estimation is one of the best men that breathes. Nobody deserves more than he does all his just debts from me, for he has been brother and father to me.' He also found the tide of practice which began to flow in on him entailed outlay, for it had increased beyond the reach of being walked over. He had to adventure more expenditure on a carriage. 'This drosky,' he explains to his brother, to account for the extravagance, 'is to save my body from excess of work when there is (as during the winter's lecturing season) little time left to devote to rest.' He had, however, close on the dawn of '40 won the wife he wished, and had a helpmate by him with whom to face these difficulties which for a brief time laid him aside by their overwhelming worries. His first lecture was delivered in November, and he insisted on Dr. Dawson of Bathgate, whom he looked on as his earliest friend, coming in to hear how the 'Bathgate bairn' would meet his class.

His session opened brilliantly. He fulfilled the expectation of his supporters, and he pleased the students. 'I am delighted, of course, with the class,' he wrote to Miss Grindlay. 'I had to apply to the Council for additional sittings, and again for some days students were standing for want of seats. For the first time in the history of the University, the Midwifery is the first— I mean the largest—class within its walls. Do you know I sometimes fancy the students have "gane gyte" when they come crushing into the room to hear *me* lecture.' His class, it was said, at once became popular. Students crowded its benches. Many even who had long passed away from College life took tickets for it, that with him they might survey those new and fresh fields of study into which he led his pupils. He drew £600 from his class his first year, but he was so keen to be free from all debt, he decided he would have to inflict boarders on himself to help the purse. He, however, was relieved when no 'paying guest' could be found to break in on his solitude of two. To quote his own words: 'My tea is so *very* cosy and comfortable when I come home at five. I do wish I might get through my difficulties without boarders, for Jessie's sake as well as my own.'

Towards the end of 1840 his eldest child was born, and he was mightily proud of this little addition to his anxieties. 'My daughter, oh my daughter! Ay, there's the rub. I do love the little Marmazette so,' he wrote. His 'little Marmazette' lightened his way for four years, and then she was snatched from him, the first of his near ones to be laid on that sunny slope of Warriston which was the first piece of landed property he owned.

Luckily the young couple, working hard, and living with studied economy to get free of debt, rejoicing over the arrival of their daughter, could not look ahead to trials and losses, for which neither fame nor wealth could compensate. The baby was christened Margaret, after her maternal grandmother.

The year of Simpson's election to the Chair, his old schoolfellow, Walter Gilchrist, reminded him, was one he would not easily forget. Gilchrist was then working as a shoemaker, but while he wrought at the last, he studied, eventually took his medical degree, and became a practitioner in Leith. He thus wrote to Simpson: 'In May 1839 you were a lodger, same month a householder; in November a candidate for *the Chair*; in December a *husband*; in February 1840 a *Professor*; in October a *father*. These were the points in your career on which my imagination lighted as I ran back over the catalogue of immediate events.'

The next years succeeding this remarkable one were marked by unwearied industry. They were successful from a monetary point of view, and he gratefully paid back his borrowings and stood unclogged by debt. He immediately moved uphill to more fashionable quarters, and one New Year's Day sent an oaken box with a set of silver spoons in it out to Bathgate to 'Mr. Alexander Simpson, Bathgate, *the best of brothers*, from J. Y. S.' This substantial proof of his brotherly love had cost some self-sacrifice to purchase, but Sandy valued them for the goodwill as well as the wealth of silver, and, as precious heirlooms, bequeathed them to his youngest son.

Busy as he was, no one enjoyed social gaieties more than the Professor, who gave such scanty hours to sleep, and so many to patient and pen. The merry meetings, the impromptu dances at his house, when he would clear the furniture out of the way, and make the self-invited guests welcome to such frugal fare as his larder held, are not yet forgotten. The very uncertainty of his presence made him all the more appreciated when he remained master of the revels. Finally, in 1845, he bought 52 Queen Street, a house so many remember, where he kept an open door and a table spread for all.

Seeing his practice increasing, he added to his purchase in his usual wholesale manner, and built rooms for patients which were never empty. His wife furnished the new home with appropriate taste.

A sense of fun and humour, a hearty enjoyment of a joke, a fondness for reeling off verses and rhymes full of light-hearted bagatelles, was a prominent trait in the Professor, and relieved the monotony of work.

Early in the forties he began to write on archæology. At the heading of one of his papers he quotes from Wordsworth what he truly found—

> 'I have owed to them,
> In hours of weariness, sensations sweet
> Felt in the blood.'

Antiquarian matters were ever a diversion and playfield to him. His first printed paper linked it to medicine—the monograph on Leper Houses read before the Medico-Chirurgical Society, and enlarged afterwards. It was a paper brimming over with notes, references, and research.

All the time that he was going through the fatigue of professional work, he was keeping his eyes and ears open for any new light on science. His rise into fame was rapid. By 1843 he writes to his brother: 'I have been exceedingly fortunate in getting the Princess (Marie Amelia of Baden, wife of the Duke of Hamilton) as a patient, because it quickly places me at the top of the practice on this side of the Tweed. She is a most unaffected, happy, laughing lassie, always pleased herself, and trying to please others also. She is the constant theme of talk in our Edinburgh circles at present, and crowds wait occasionally in the streets to see her. The Marchioness of Breadalbane and the Countess of Lincoln are likewise located in the Palace under my professional care, and the old Palace is quite converted into an hospital.' In 1845 he went to a historic house in London to attend a future duchess, and he writes home: 'My advent in London this time certainly is a very different one from what it was, not so many years ago. Yesterday I took a stroll out, and bought the enclosed Life of me, published on the day of my arrival. They were all very kind to me, and my rooms look into St. James's Park, with one of the prettiest views in London. The family are all good, lovable, plain folks. I sat down to dinner with a duke, two marquises, and two other lords.' He had, even before he moved into Queen Street, some aristocratic patients, for one who so short a time before had only 'some very poor and penniless patients to employ him.' But whether in palace or in the 'lands' in the Old Town, his heart was wrung with pity for the sufferings he saw. He believed one of his duties as a physician was to battle against pain. Practice had come to him. His fame was known over 'broad Scotland.' His debts were paid; and though he had wife and children dependent on him, he saw he could now provide for them. He had his way clear, therefore, to take the next step in his career, which, as a writer in a London paper said, secured him the honour of being 'the greatest conqueror in human history; and his triumphs, instead of being bought by weeping and anguish, have stayed floods of tears, and prevented a world of agony'—or, as a poet said of him after his death—

> 'Great in his art, and peerless in resource,
>   He strove the fiend of human pain to quell;
> Nor ever champion dared so bold a course
>   With truer heart or weapons proved so well.'

In 1847 the Duchess of Sutherland wrote telling him that the Queen had appointed him one of Her Majesty's physicians for Scotland, which, to quote from the letter in question, 'his high character and abilities make him fit for.' To his brother, to whom he ever hastened to communicate his successes, he said, 'Flattery *from* the Queen is perhaps not common flattery; but I am far less interested in it than in having delivered a woman this week *without* any pain while inhaling sulphuric ether. I can think of naught else.' He had climbed to a position of eminence up the 'stey brae' of success, and the time had now come when, untrammelled by debt and difficulties, he was ready to enter the lists and fight against the Giant Pain.

CHAPTER IV

CHLOROFORM

'The sad world blesseth thee.'—*Light of Asia.*

VERY early in his student days he had so sickened at the suffering he witnessed in the operating theatre, that he had shrunk from the scene, decided to abandon his medical studies, and seek his way in the paths of law. But he turned slowly again from the Parliament House, with its 'interminable pattering of legal feet,' back to the Infirmary, for he knew it was cowardly to desert the colours under which he had enrolled. Like the true soldier he was, he determined to use such powers as had been granted him to fight a good fight, more especially against 'that foretaste and small change of death—pain.' As his profession led him into constant scenes of suffering, his resolve was never forgotten. His eagerness for work, the struggle at the commencement of his career, did not obliterate it.

When, in 1836, he got the house-surgeonship of the Lying-in Hospital at Leith, in some letters he asked: 'Cannot something be done to render the patient unconscious while under acute pain, without interfering with the free and healthy play of the natural functions?' He turned his attention to mesmerism. He at once began to study it, to see if such phenomena may be tamed and yoked, and made to work for human good. 'I was a great sceptic four weeks ago,' he wrote to Sandy, 'and laughed at it all, but have seen enough to stagger me. Yesterday I magnetised a young woman by waving my hand only in a looking-glass, *behind her back*, in which her shadow was reflected, and she was so sound asleep in three minutes that you could not wake her by pinching or rugging at her as severely as you pleased. I have had all the principal medical men here seeing it done at my hospital.' He found people easily amenable to mesmerism, through their own imagination as well as his conjuring presence. An insomnia patient came to him and he informed her: 'I leave to-morrow for London, but if you think of me at the appointed time, I shall bring on sleep in the usual way.' He forgot his promise, but she went asleep at the hour arranged. Another patient he could render dumb when he willed, and, at his table, forbade her to speak till he gave her leave. He was called out of the room, went off hurriedly on a journey, and came home some days after, to find her speechless and furious, having to express her anger in writing. He hurried off, travel-stained and tired, to give her back the use of her tongue, and she poured reproaches so volubly on him that he fled. He did not proceed very far in his experiments with mesmerism, which he saw could unduly influence weaker minds; but he was always on the outlook for some new remedy.

In 1846 there came from America the news of the first trial of ether in surgery, and no one hailed it more heartily than Professor Simpson, who was the first man to use it in his own line of practice. The history of anæsthesia, my father said, 'always took me a full hour in my lecture,' and it is not only from the Morton-Wells trials in the 'forties' that it takes its rise. The 'deep sleep' into which Adam was cast, Professor Simpson remarked, was the first notice of an anæsthetic he could find. Helen of Troy used some drug called Nepenthe, which, Homer tells us, when Ulysses and his companions drank of it in their wine, 'frees them from grief and from anger, and causes oblivion of all ills.' This concoction the Grecian beauty learned from a daughter of Egypt. Theocritus spoke of a mesmeric charm which deadened the senses. 'That author,' wrote Sir James, 'calls this insensibility to pain *nodynia* (νωδῦνία), which is a better word than anæsthesia, and I have often regretted not adopting it, rather than the latter.' A preparation made from Indian hemp was familiar to the Chinese 1500 years ago, and in 700 B.C., the 'wine of the condemned,' alluded to by Amos, is surmised to have been also of Indian hemp. A surgeon in the twelfth century, one Hugo de Lucca, used a sponge soaked in a mixture, of which mandragora was an ingredient, and it was held to the patient's nose to render him unconscious. He describes, too, how to revive the patient after the operation. 'This being finished, in order to awaken him, apply another sponge, dipped in vinegar, frequently to the nose, or throw the juice of the root of fenugrek into the nostrils; shortly he awakens.' This specific, not improved on, was abandoned, as it frequently happened he did not return to consciousness or reason.

In our own country, in the Middle Ages, drugs that produced a 'show of death' were evidently known to cunning herbalists, for in the ballad, 'The Gay

Gosshawk,' the heroine is dosed like Shakespeare's Juliet. Towards the close of the sixteenth century, Paré mentions that drugs which stole away the senses had been resorted to by former surgeons.

> 'I'll imitate the pities of old surgeons
> To this lost limb—who, ere they show their art,
> Cast one asleep, then cut the diseased part,'

wrote Middleton, 1617, showing that the memory of the early narcotics still dwelt in men's minds. In 1784, Dr. Moore tried to annul pain during an operation by compressing the nerves beforehand. The big stride anæsthesia made was in Sir Humphrey Davy's hands, with his application of nitrous oxide. 'It appears,' he wrote, 'capable of destroying physical pain. It may be used with advantage during surgical operations in which no great effusion of blood takes place.' 'The first experiment,' says Sir James, 'of breathing a vapour to such an extent as to destroy sensibility, was neither made in America nor in our own days. Without adverting to the acknowledged fact that it was accomplished with the vapours driven off from hypnotic vegetable extracts by the older surgeons, from Hugo de Lucca and Theodoric downwards, let me remind you that Sir Humphrey Davy boldly—and notwithstanding he had witnessed occasional deaths in animals from it—made the experiment many times upon himself, in the last century, with nitrous oxide, and, further, found that headache and other pains disappeared under its influence.' The uses of this gas lay partially dormant for nearly forty years, till a Mr. Colton, lecturing on laughing-gas in Hartford, Connecticut, had among his audience Mr. Horace Wells, dentist. Mr. Wells was struck by seeing a person, who inhaled it, fall and bruise himself badly, without being conscious of the fact. Next day Mr. Colton administered the gas to Mr. Wells, and a Dr. Rigg extracted his tooth. 'A new era in tooth-pulling!' he exclaimed. 'It did not hurt me more than the prick of a pin.' This was the first anæsthetic operation in America, 1844. He was unsuccessful in an attempt at painless dentistry in public, at Boston, and was hissed. He left disheartened, unaware that his failure was owing to not giving a sufficiently full dose. In 1818, in the journal published by the Royal Institution (London), the case of a man who, by imprudent inhalation of the vapour of ether, was rendered unconscious for thirty hours, is mentioned. Faraday in this country, and Godman in America, showed, as the result of their observation and experience, that the effects of the inhalation of the vapour of sulphuric ether were quite similar on the nervous system to those produced by the inhalation of the vapour of nitrous oxide gas. This vapour of ether was used across the Atlantic by Crawford Long, in Georgia, in 1842. While he waited to test its powers, Morton, a clever and daring young dentist, wanted some nitrous oxide gas to proceed on Wells' line. Mr. Jackson, to whom he appealed, and who was more of a scientist than Morton, recommended ether. In 1846, Morton pluckily inhaled it, and saw, when he recovered consciousness, he had been some eight minutes insensible. He quickly grasped the idea that longer operations than tooth-drawing could be accomplished by its means. He begged for a public trial of it at Massachusetts General Hospital, 30th September 1846; and as Oliver Wendell Holmes said, ' By this priceless gift to humanity, the fierce extremity of suffering has been steeped in the waters of forgetfulness, and the deepest furrow in the knotted brow of agony has been smoothed for ever.' In a letter to Morton, November 19, 1847, Professor Simpson says: 'Of course the great thought is that of producing insensibility, and for that the world is, I think, indebted to you.' The claims of Wells and Jackson *versus* Morton immediately cropped up, but have nothing to do with this history. Their story is a sad one of disappointments, of trouble, of sudden death, and it is curious that America was long unkind to those sons of hers who took the initiative step in raising Sir Humphrey Davy's suggestion from its dormant state.

James Simpson never looked doubtingly askance at the march of progress. He was always the first to stride with it. He notes: 'The first case of midwifery in which sulphuric ether was adopted as an anæsthetic occurred here under my care on January 19, 1847, and was soon afterwards reported in the journals of the day.' He set to work to bring ether into use in obstetric practice, and with this aim in view he wrote pamphlets which he spread broadcast, but he found conservative opposition to innovations hindering the adoption of the boon. All through the summer, with his usual prodigious energy, he was in hot pursuit of a better 'drowsy syrup' than ether. Explaining his object, he says: 'Latterly, in order to avoid, if possible, some of the inconveniences pertaining to sulphuric ether, particularly its disagreeable and persistent smell, its occasional tendency to irritation of the bronchi during its first inspirations, and the large quantity of it required to be used (more especially in protracted cases of labour), I have tried upon myself and others the inhalation of different other volatile fluids, with the hope that some one of them might be found to possess the advantages of ether without its disadvantages. For this purpose I selected for experiment, and have inhaled, several chemical liquids, of a more fragrant or agreeable odour, such as chloride of hydro-carbon, etc. Then Mr. Waldie, a Linlithgowshire man, first named perchloride of formyle as worthy among others of a trial.' Nightly, when the day's work was over, my father and his assistants, Dr. George Keith and Dr. Matthews Duncan, through the summer and autumn of 1847, tried various narcotic drugs 'which shall ever medicine thee to such sweet sleep.' Mr. Waldie promised to send the one he recommended, but it did not come, and Duncan & Flockhart supplied it.

Contemporary accounts as to its first trial differ slightly. Dr. George Keith and my aunt, Miss Grindlay, are the only two survivors. My aunt says the Professor came into the dining-room one afternoon, holding a little bottle in his hand, and saying, 'This will turn the world upside down.' He then poured some into a tumbler, breathed it, and fell unconscious. This may have been some other drug, for many were tried, but till recently, when dimmed by age, Miss Grindlay's memory was a veracious one. Miss Petrie, her niece, was much at Queen Street in these days, and in a journal she kept, mentions that my father 'tried everything on himself first,' and once, after swallowing some concoction, was insensible for two hours. Dr. Keith recalled another experiment, when, not content with chloroform, he tried a compound of carbon, which brought on such irritation in breathing that he had to be kept under chloroform to relieve him. In experimenting upon himself, he was ever 'bold even to rashness,' as Sir Lyon Playfair (now Lord Playfair) in 1883 asserted of him in the House of Commons. He was speaking of vivisection, and told how Sir James, still searching for something better, came to his laboratory, and Playfair put in his hand a new liquid. He wanted to inhale it there and then, but Playfair insisted on two rabbits being first dosed with it, and they speedily succumbed. 'Now, was not this,' he asked the House, 'a justifiable experiment on animals? Was not it worth the sacrifice of two rabbits to save the life of the most distinguished physician of his time, who by the introduction of chloroform has done so much to mitigate animal suffering?'

Seeing he was ever recklessly rash in regard to himself, it is not unlikely he may have had a private trial of chloroform, and laid it aside again, to start fair with his two assistants, who had worked so unflinchingly with him. Some other compounds were tried that night, and then chloroform, which was lying in its little phial among some papers, was unearthed, and the result of this, its first trial as an anæsthetic, 4th November 1847, is best described in Professor Simpson's own words in a letter to Mr. Waldie, who had previously drawn his attention to this heavy-smelling 'perchloride of formyle.'

'I am sure you will be delighted to see part of the good results of our hasty conversation. I had the chloroform for several days in the house before trying it, as, after seeing it such a heavy, unvolatile-like liquid, I despaired of it, and went on dreaming about others. The first night we took it, Dr. Duncan, Dr. Keith, and I all tried it simultaneously, and were all "under the table" in a minute or two.' Dr. George Keith, writing to me in 1891, says: 'Dr. Miller, in the appendix to his work on surgery, published soon after, gives a full account of the scene. It is pretty correct, only he says we all took the chloroform at once. This, with a new substance to try, would have been foolish, and the fact is, I began to inhale it a few minutes before the others. On seeing the effects on me, and hearing my approval before I went quite over, they both took a dose, and I believe we were all more or less under the table together, much to the alarm of your mother, who was present.' Professor Miller, his neighbour, who used to come in every morning to see if the experimenters had survived, says: 'These experiments were performed after the long day's toil was over, at late night or early morn, and when the greater part of mankind were soundly anæsthetised in the arms of common sleep.' He describes how, after a 'weary day's labour,' the trio sat down and inhaled various drugs out of tumblers, as was their custom, and chloroform was searched for and 'found beneath a heap of waste paper, and with each tumbler newly charged, the inhalers resumed their occupation. . . . A moment more, then all was quiet, and then a crash. On awakening, Dr. Simpson's first perception was mental. "This is far stronger and better than ether," said he to himself. His second was to note that he was prostrate on the floor, and that among the friends about him there was both confusion and alarm. Of his assistants, Dr. Duncan he saw snoring heavily, and Dr. Keith kicking violently at the table above him. They made several more trials of it that eventful evening, and were so satisfied with the results that the festivities of the evening did not terminate till a late hour, 3 A.M.'

The onlookers to this scene were my mother, her sister Miss Grindlay, her niece Miss Petrie, and her brother-in-law Captain Petrie. Accustomed as they had grown to experiments, they were startled with the results of this first 'inhaling of chloroform.' My aunt often spoke of Dr. Keith's ghastly expression when, ceasing to kick, he raised his head to the level of the table and stared with unconscious eyes on them. She had such a horror of chloroform, she refused ever to try it. My father used to threaten to put her under its influence, and when she fled he gave chase; but, light of foot as he was in these days, she always escaped, for fits of laughter used to seize him and choke him off the pursuit. Great was my father's joy at his success, and in having, in so handy a form, so potent an agent to deaden the suffering he had daily to witness.

The Duchess of Argyll expressed his feelings in a letter she wrote before chloroform was a month old: 'Dear Dr. Simpson, I cannot resist one line to wish you joy of your discovery. I think your life must be a very happy one from the relief of *not* witnessing pain, which it must be as painful to see as to bear. It must make you very happy, dear sir, to have discovered so great a boon. Next to the cure of souls, there can be no more wonderful blessing bestowed on man than to have been allowed the possession of such a "gift of healing."'

The half-ounce the experimenters had, on that evening

when 'they were all under the mahogany in a trice,' as my father said in another letter of that time, was soon used, and Mr. Hunter of Duncan & Flockhart had to work hard with an ordinary retort to manufacture sufficient to supply the demand from 52 Queen Street. The partners sat up till 2 A.M. to brew the first perchloride of formyle Professor Simpson used; and this was the beginning of their great chloroform works, in which now, so great is the increase of its use, that three-quarters of a million doses were in 1895 made *weekly*.

The first woman put under the influence of this new agent was Miss Petrie, my mother's niece, she boldly trying it on the evening of its new birth. The first child born under its influence was the daughter of a medical contemporary of Professor Simpson's, and she was christened Anæsthesia to commemorate the fact, as the first child in all the Russias that was vaccinated was named Vaccinoff. Anæsthesia, when she grew to be sweet seventeen, was photographed, and sent her likeness to the Professor, above whose desk it hung, for he was very proud of chloroform's first-born. The initiatory public test of chloroform was held on the 15th November 1847, within the Infirmary, where James Simpson as a student had sickened at and shrunk from the sight of others' suffering. A previous trial had been arranged for, but press of work detained my father from keeping his appointment, or the 'divinity which shapes our ends' had put obstacles in his way, for the operation went on without him, and the patient died on the first incision of the knife, so chloroform's reputation was saved. One of the three cases on which a few days later it was tried was one in which ether could not have been used. Another of these early patients, a soldier, approved so highly of 'the overture to the swooning dream of chloroform,' that on his emergence from it, after the operation, 'he seized the sponge, with which administration had been made, and, thrusting it into his mouth, again resumed inhalation more vigorously than before, as if it were too good a thing to be stopped so soon.' At this public trial M. Dumas was present, 'and was in no small degree rejoiced to witness the wonderful physiological effects of a substance with whose chemical history his own name was so intimately connected.' Perchloride of formyle was first discovered and described at nearly the same time by Soubeiran (1831) and Liebig (1832), but its composition was first accurately ascertained by the distinguished French chemist, Dumas, in 1835.

It was intended for internal use. The go-ahead spirit and the promptitude of the man who discovered the narcotic powers of the drug is testified by the facts that the first trial of chloroform took place on November 4th, by the 10th he had lectured on it to the Medico-Chirurgical Society, and issued a pamphlet on its merits, so as to spread what he believed to be 'tidings of great joy,' unhampered by patent, free to all. But the tidings were coldly received. Prejudice, and the crippling determination to walk only in timeworn paths and to eschew new ways, rose up against it, and did their best to smother the new-found blessing. It is curious to look back now on the fiercely fanatical opposition which, half a century ago, assailed the means to lull pain. It was in vain people were told that not only was agony saved, but that the distress of mind before, and the shock to the system during, operations would save life as well as suffering; or to draw attention to the fact that the surgeon's hand was steadier, the operation more dexterously and deliberately done, when he knew the inert patient was freed from the extremity of anguish his knife inflicted.

Professor Simpson not only found an anæsthetic safer, more manageable, and more effectual than ether, but he had to fight for its use. The profession and the world, though they prayed for freedom from suffering, would not avail themselves of the means put into their hands. Their narrow, warped minds suspected quackery. Professor Miller says: 'It fills me with indignation to find that there are in some quarters attempts being made to prejudice the profession, and especially the public, against anæsthesia, and to make it appear as if chloroform, having already run its short day's course, had been quietly gathered to the tomb of all ephemeral innovations. The same opposition has always met the great advances of truth, yet it has not retarded such onward movement long. And I gladly make them over to my friend and colleague, who may be said to be the *maternal* parent of this anæsthetic.' He could claim that title, for in America, at a public meeting, they said of him: 'There are none of us that have not, through ourselves, or through those that are dearer than ourselves, been the partakers of the bounty that his courage and science have given to humanity, who through him have had the terrible pains of maternity relieved, if not destroyed.' Then Sir James Paget in 1879 says: 'But there were other great pains yet to be prevented, the pains of childbirth. For escape from these, honour and deep gratitude are due to Sir James Simpson. No energy or knowledge or power of language less than his would have overcome the fears that the insensibility, which was proved to be harmless in surgical operations and their consequences, should be often fatal or very mischievous in parturition. And to these fears were added a crowd of pious protests (raised for the most part by men) against so gross an interference as this seemed, with the ordained course of human nature. Simpson, with equal force of words and work, beat all down, and by his adoption of chloroform as a substitute for ether, promoted the whole use of anæsthetics.'

The amount of bigotry and baneful obstinacy and abuse the profession and the older folks among the public brought to bear upon Simpson, astonished him, but he stubbornly continued his struggle. 'I feel,' he wrote, 'that the greater the good I can accomplish for my profession and humanity, the greater will always be the temporary blame attempted to be heaped on me by the bigoted portion of the profession.' But if he got volleys of vituperation from those who were opposed to him, he was on the other hand pleased by letters from many who sat in high places, and who encouraged him by unstinted praise. He knew their example would help vastly to break down the barriers of ignorance and narrow-minded objections. 'You will be pleased to hear the Queen had chloroform administered to her during her late confinement. Her Majesty was greatly pleased with the effect, and she certainly never has had a better recovery,' wrote one of Her Majesty's physicians from London.

A storm of invective rose against the new anodyne, on the ground that it undermined religion. Many of the clergy held that to try to remove the primal curse on women was to fight against divine law. 'An esteemed clerical friend, in writing me,' said the Professor, 'stated he was afraid *his* cloth was perhaps even more sinful than ours, if this outrageous view were true; for the introduction of sin was the consequence of the Fall, and the Church, in labouring to banish and abrogate that effect, in trying to turn mankind from sin, were actually trying to cancel the greatest and most undoubted effects of the first curse upon the human race.'

In the paper my father wrote on 'The Defence of Anæsthesia,' against the scriptural objections, he quoted from James iv. 7 : 'Therefore to him that knoweth to do good and doeth it not, to him it is sin.' In this last-named pamphlet he set forth that if we followed the letter of the word without the spirit thereof, not only would the daughters of Eve have to obey the law and suffer, but the sons of Adam 'must adhere literally also to the decree of the curse, and hence must earn their bread by "the sweat of their face," and by that only.' 'In regard to the primary curse,' he writes in a letter at this period, 'the word translated "sorrow" is truly "labour," "toil," and in the very next verse the very same word means this. Adam was to eat of the ground with "sorrow." That does not mean *physical* pain, and it was cursed to bear thorns and thistles which we pull up without dreaming that it is a sin. Besides, Christ in dying surely hath "borne our griefs and carried our sorrows," and removed "the curse of the law, being made a curse for us." We may rest fully and perfectly assured that whatever is true in point of fact, or humane, and merciful in point of practice, will find no condemnation in the Word of God. His mission was to introduce mercy, not sacrifice.' 'Is it not against nature to take away the pangs of labour?' an Irish lady asked him. 'Is it not,' he answered, 'unnatural for you to have been carried over from Ireland in a steamboat against wind and tide?' To a medical contemporary who objected to chloroform he replied, 'It does nothing but *save pain*, you allege. A carriage does nothing but save fatigue. Which is most important to get done away with? Your fatigue, or your patient's screams and tortures? To confess to you the truth, my blood feels chilled by the inhumanity and deliberate cruelty which you and some members of your profession openly avow. And I know that you will yet, in a few years, look back with horror at your present resolution of refusing to relieve your patients, merely because you have not yet had time to get rid of some old professional caprices and nonsensical thoughts upon the subject.'

A French physiologist, M. Magendie, held 'it was a trivial matter to suffer, and a discovery, whose object was to prevent pain, was of a slight interest only.' Others persisted that the cold steel of the surgeon was a good tonic. On the other hand, Dr. Gooch said, 'Mere pain can destroy life'; and another surgeon vouched 'that pain, when amounting to a certain degree of intensity and duration, is of itself destructive. It exhausts the principles of life.' Professor Simpson gathered statistics to show that chloroform saved life, as it saved the shock to the nerves and system before, as well as during, an operation.

Mr. John Bell reminds us in his works: 'Without reading the books of these old surgeons, it is not possible to imagine the horrors of the cautery, nor how much reason Paré had for upbraiding the surgeons of his own time with their cruelties. The horrors of the patient and his ungovernable cries, the hurry of the operators and assistants, the sparkling of the heated irons, and the hissing of the blood against them, *must* have been terrible scenes, and surgery *must* in those days have been a horrid trade.' Even with the improvements of the first half of the nineteenth century, the operating theatre was a nightmare before it was revolutionised by chloroform: 'one of God's greatest blessings to His suffering children,' as Dr. John Brown called it in *Rab*.

Even the blessing of being able to render the patient unconscious by this narcotic, in his own bed, and thus conveying him into the operating room, saves abhorrent scenes. Professor Miller recalls the olden days when a patient, in a panic of fear, was being removed from the ward: 'His progress might be traced by frightful yellings, or, at least, by sobs of deep distress, and occasionally a number of stout assistants scarcely sufficed to prevent on the way a self-effected rescue and escape. All this was bad, painful, injurious, unseemly. All such scenes are now unknown.' To lead people to use chloroform, Professor Simpson received a letter from Dr. George Wilson, who had undergone an operation before the days of anæsthesia, in which he describes his anxiety of mind thinking of what lay before him, what he suffered by the surgeon's knife, till he saw 'the bloody, dismembered limb lying on the floor.' 'The particular pangs are now forgotten,' he wrote, 'but the black whirlwind of emotion, the horror of great darkness, the sense of desertion by God and man, bordering close upon despair, which swept through my mind and overwhelmed my heart, I can never forget, however gladly I would do so. Even now, if by some Lethean draught I could erase the remembrances of that time, I would drink it.'

In 1853 it was said that some deaths were directly due to the use of chloroform. Again the Professor collected statistics and wrote in its defence, proving how its use had lessened the death-rate, and how the reported fatal cases were either fictitious, as he found was the case with many of the deaths attributed to it, or were due to quite other causes. He also drew attention to the fact that bad chloroform was used, and not administered properly. 'A large, full, *rapid* dose of it at once' was his prescription, and he had not a single death. 'I am not aware of any death in Scotland or elsewhere from the use of chloroform in midwifery, out of the many thousands of cases in which it has now been employed in the Old and New World,' he said. In another paper he drew attention to the many accidents caused by the use of steam, in factories and on railways, yet, would people give it up because of these? Again, opium, and other drugs of greatest service to humanity, by improper doses claimed many annual victims, yet no one had so little sense left as to propose that their use should be discontinued. Two million of doses of chloroform were then annually manufactured by one firm alone in Edinburgh, and he asks: 'Is there any other common or potent drug which could be given in full doses in two million of instances per annum with greater impunity?' To show how few fatalities it caused, Dr. George Otis, U.S. Army, said: 'Ether is not suited for use on the battlefield, because it is impossible for the attendants to carry an adequate quantity upon the actual field; whereas a surgeon may take on his person, in a flask, a sufficient quantity of chloroform to produce anæsthesia in all the cases he is likely to be called upon to attend. You well know the history of the use of chloroform in the Crimean and Italian campaigns, where it was employed without a single disaster, and I am informed by Langenbeck and Stromeyer that a similar result attended the seven weeks' Austro-Prussian war. In our own unhappy struggle, chloroform was administered in more than one hundred and twenty thousand cases, and I am unable to learn of more than *eight* cases in which a fatal result can be traceable to its use.'

Good as he found chloroform, Professor Simpson had always a hope he might find something more efficacious, and often risked his own life trying to discover a still better means to banish pain. He was found insensible in his room by his servant Clarke. 'He'll kill himsel' yet wi' thae expeeriments, an' he's a big fule, for they'll never find onything better than chlory,' said the man, as they anxiously tried to waken the Professor from his Lethean sleep. His butler's words, however, roused him. The honest butler himself tried experimenting. Seeing the Professor and his friends trying to induce unconsciousness by drinking a mixture of champagne and chloroform, Clarke had hurried downstairs and given the cook 'a richt gude willy-waught' of the draught. The result was, the woman fell flat on the floor, which sent Clarke flying upstairs, crying, 'Come doon, come doon, Doctor! I've pushioned the cook deid.' 'I tell ye, chlory's the best,' Clarke persisted; and he was so far right, for as yet, on the eve of its jubilee, it has had no supplanter, though doubtless in the coming century 'Light, more light' will be shed on anæsthesia.

At the meeting of the British Medical Congress in 1890, Mr. Lawson Tait put clearly before this generation the hard battle the Professor had fought. 'We are apt to ignore the fact that all our brilliant advancement to-day could never have been arrived at but for chloroform. We could not have developed the splendid work of the modern ophthalmic surgeon, and the modern development of abdominal surgery never would have been dreamed of, but for the genius and indomitable fighting qualities of James Young Simpson, who threshed out the victory of anæsthesia, and gave us the anæsthetic which has held its own against all comers.' Also in 1895, in the *Times*, the same gentleman, after reviewing the delicate operations now accomplished, says: 'But where should we have been without anæsthetics? No human being could undergo, in a conscious state, such operations as I have spoken of: I doubt if any human being could nerve himself to perform them. At the head of the list for whom I claim the true credit, I place the name of Simpson, the greatest genius our profession has produced for centuries. *He fought the fight of anæsthesia.*'

Professor Simpson doggedly fought on till he won his victory. His triumph over human suffering he always regarded as his greatest achievement. When a title came to him, late in life, he took for his crest the healing rod of Æsculapius, and for his motto '*Victo Dolore*,' in recollection of the struggle he had waged against pain and prejudice. His last fight for chloroform was on his deathbed. In accepting the freedom of the City of Edinburgh, the Lord Provost, Dr. William Chambers, thanked him for the greatest of all discoveries in modern times, 'the application of chloroform to the assuagement of human suffering.' Sir James replied in an impromptu speech, and Dr. Bigelow, Boston, U.S.A., was indignant at him for having shut out the American hemisphere from the credit of the discovery. In reply, as he too prophetically said, 'This is my last attempt at professional writing,' he set forth how he never claimed to have discovered the anæsthetic properties of sulphuric ether, but of chloroform, and also reminded his American brothers how he had fought for the use of any anæsthetic. But before the letter crossed the Atlantic, the cable had flashed the news that he had conquered pain for ever. His transatlantic medical comrades paid him a graceful tribute. When the news of his death came to them, the Gynæcological Society of Boston held a memorial meeting in honour of their 'late beloved associate,' who was, they said, 'one of nature's noblemen.' Above the altar the flags of America and Britain hung, and on a silver laurel wreath bearing his monogram was written: '*Fuit ubique in terris est in cœlo.*'

CHAPTER V

APPEARANCE—POPULARITY—SYMPATHY

> 'A heart that beats
> In all its pulses with the common heart
> Of human kind, which the same things make glad,
> The same make sorry.'
>
> *From the French.*

IN a letter to 'his Mary,' in the forties, he says: 'I have been at a loss what little article to send you out by Mr. Broadwood. At last I had the presumption to fix upon a daguerreotype portrait of myself, as being easily carried, and probably you would value it at times, as a remembrance of a rascal who owes his own dearest sister so much, so very, *very* much.' This early sun-picture was taken in a wooden shed at the foot of the Mound. The photographer was surprised at the haste of his sitter, who begged him to 'Come away, quick now! It shouldn't take a minute to do.' The stranger, after hurriedly searching his pockets for small money, left a five-pound note in payment, with orders to send the change to 52 Queen Street with the likeness, and then was off again full speed along Princes Street. As to what manner of man he was in appearance at that time, though sculptor and painter have immortalised him, he was a difficult person to describe, for his most striking qualities were in his expression. He had in repose a somewhat melancholy, but ever pleasing face. 'No one with a brain and a heart,' said Longfellow, 'can be happy;' and on Sir James's face was graven, as our late poet said—

> 'The heavy and the weary weight
> Of all this unintelligible world.'

It is also as hard a task to give any idea to those who knew him not, of his lovableness and attractiveness. A word-of-mouth description of him in youth came down to us from an old wife at Bathgate, who spoke of him as a 'bonnie bairn, wi' rosy cheek and dimpled mou'.' The rosy cheek paled when the flush of childhood was over, the dimples remained uneradicated by the long sad lines which sufferings and sorrows ploughed down his face. His first portrait in oil was done by Sir William Fettes-Douglas, when he was a newly-made Professor, to send to one he called 'My Jessie's mother.' In it he is represented as a firmly built man with broad shoulders, slimmer than those who knew him later would have believed him to have been, with a thick thatch of auburn hair surrounding the face, which, except for the deep carvings of time, was little altered. His surtout and choker in '40 are of the identical cut he wore in '70. A book, as usual, is in his hand. 'I hunger for a book,' he wrote to Mary, 'and I thirst for time to read.' The hands which held the book were peculiar, a curious combination of strength and delicacy of character. They were extraordinarily broad and powerful, but the fingers were pointed and specially sensitive of touch. In him were realised John Bell's four ideals of the perfect Æsculapius: 'The brain of an *Apollo*, the eye of an *Eagle*, the heart of a *Lion*, and the hand of a *Lady*.' He never could endure touching any gritty, grating substance with his soft, full, cushioned fingers. His breadth made his stature appear less in height than it really was, but he had a goodly presence, which made him, when on a platform alongside some veritable 'sons of Anak,' remain undwarfed by their superior height. 'Who is that remarkable man?' asked an English tourist of his Edinburgh hotelkeeper, as the Professor passed him. 'You will never forget him,' replied the man, enlarging on the doctor's popularity, 'now you've once seen him.' The tourist, thirty years after, told me he still in his mind's eye could distinctly recall him, for his unique presence in a few moments was indelibly imprinted on his memory. What was said of Fénélon might be truly said of Sir James: 'He was cast in a particular mould never used for anybody else.'

In 1853 a newspaper thus describes him: 'In stature the Professor is somewhat under the middle size. The roundness of his whole form and the absence of Scotch "processes of bone" would authorise the inference of English extraction. His ambrosial locks, dark and almost imperceptibly shaded with red, fall upon his shoulders. No feature in the Professor's countenance is overgrown. The forehead is broad and projecting rather than lofty. There is much firmness about the mouth and the lips. The eye is brilliant, and looks out from the eyebrows with an energy and penetration betraying great mental power. With the fiercer radiation of its eagle fires is blended the soft glow of a warm heart, which gives it a decided intellectual and moral expression. There is a fascination in his air, manners, and conversation, an irresistible moral gravitation which elicits and wins the admiration, love, and confidence of all who come within the magic circle of its influence.'

His tenderness of heart shone out of his eyes—eyes so changeful and so deep-set that it was difficult to name their colour. In these 'windows of the soul' there was always the same steadfastness and sunny genialness. 'Loquacious eyes,' someone called them, 'changing with the emotion of the moment,' full of sympathy or drollery, as one after another of his guests possessed his attention. His mouth, mobile like his eyes, could be stern at times, but melted into sympathetic smiles when anything to please or to pity caught his attention. This combination of firmness and gentleness, so clearly written on his face, had been a good letter of introduction to him throughout life. 'The head of Jove, the body of Bacchus,' said Gerald Massey of him.

He never seemed to get flurried, but with a leisurely brevity compassed much. In 1848 a medical man thus graphically pictured him in an Indian paper: 'Decidedly the most wonderful man of the age in which he lives is Simpson of Edinburgh. Nothing baffles his intellect, nothing escapes his penetrating glance, he sticks at nothing, he bungles nothing. From all parts, not of Britain only, but of Europe, do ladies rush to see, consult, and fee the little man. He has spread joy through many a rich man's house by enabling his wife to present him with a *living* child, a feat which none but Simpson ever *dared* to enable her to do. He is bold, but not reckless; ever ready, but never rash. He is prepared for every contingency, and meets it on the instant. What other men would speculate as to the propriety of for hours, Simpson *does* in a minute or two. As to ether and chloroform, they seem like invisible intelligences doomed to obey his bidding, familiars who do his work because they must, never venturing to produce effects one iota greater or less than he desires.'

His hair turned grizzled as he grew older, but remained as thick as ever; his face became sadder as trials thickened on him, but his own heartsoreness only made him more quick to respond to trouble in others. His daily routine of life, without his endless love of research, he records in a letter to his sister—a letter which has come back from Australia after forty years. 'I often wish you here, my own *dear* sister Mary, to see and share in all the honours and happiness that the world chooses to lavish on my undeserving head. My day's work at present is hurry from morning to night. I generally rise about eight, sometimes at six, or earlier, when urgent letters, new lectures, and addresses have to be written. We breakfast, 8.30. I see any patients that may come here, or receive messages, and afterwards drive off to see folks at their own houses at 9.30. I lecture at the College from 11 to 12; see hospital patients or others in the Old Town; walk here [Albany Street] to lunch at one, drive off immediately again to visit sick folk, and generally get here to dinner, or, what I like better, tea, "tousie west-country tea," about five.

Then Maggie and Davie come down for fun and frolic. After an hour's rest I am generally off again, walking always at night, unless distances are such as to require a hackney, and then home to an egg or other supper about eleven or later. Some book is generally devoured with supper, and a few minutes afterwards I am asleep, but ready to wake and start at the slightest tinkle of the night bell. Such is the usual course of each day's work during the present winter's session, varied occasionally by going out for a few hours to dinner, which I avoid as much as possible, because I always enjoy myself most at home, or by having a friend or two in here.'

The routine of his days changed little from '44, when this letter was sent to Australia, except to become busier and fuller, never to sit down alone to breakfast or lunch, and to move his gradually belating dinner-hour on to 6.30. He tried to keep that meal private to his household and himself, with the exception of an intimate friend or two with whom he wished to chat. He also, in regard to his own *menu*, adhered to the plain tastes in which he had been upreared, drinking 'honest water,' and preferring homely dishes.

He made allowance for others not having his plain tastes. Whenever he sent word home he had asked several people to dine with him, it was understood he wished *menu* and wine of the best for them, not for display, but to do honour to his guests, for he was a princely host. A well-known and now titled doctor in Edinburgh told me, when he was a new-fledged M.D., he was studying in Paris, when, hearing a door open, he looked up, and saw Sir James's broad figure filling the doorway. 'Put up your books,' he said to the student, 'and come and take me round the hospitals.' When they had done so, Sir James turned to his late pupil and said, 'Now, find out some other Edinburgh medicals, and all come and dine with me.' They came, and found a sumptuous dinner and a genial host awaiting them. Sir James remembered when Mr. Maclagan and he were in Paris in 1835. They had not many regal dinners, and he was glad he could give one to later-day students.

Busy as he ever was, he never lost his enjoyment of any diversion. A joke, a humorous story, a droll prank, he lent a ready ear and a ready laugh to. It was a great relaxation.

'And his happiness at such times!' said Miss Dunlop in *Anent Old Edinburgh*,—'gladness covered him about as with a garment!—and his laughter, especially at a good story!—it was a sight to see as well as a sound to hear, for from the crown of his head to the sole of his foot he seemed to laugh all over; but reading now of his life and overwork, it seems to us that his leisure and his laughter had only been condensed and taken strong.'

He held practical joking was wrong, and could tell gruesome tales of its evil effects, landing its victims in asylums, etc.; but with a curl of mischief lurking in the corner of his eye, and the dimples not smoothed out from his sometimes pathetically sad face, he would suggest an effective but harmless bogle-trap, and keep the victim talking while it was being prepared. He used to tell us how as a boy, he determined to frighten his sister, by seizing her in the dark and scaring her into the belief he was a robber. She screamed, and he, getting frightened at her lusty yells, held the harder and 'skirled' too. The biter was the worse bit that day.

He heard more of weeping, however, than of laughter, for his walk in life led him often into 'death's dark vale,' and his ready sympathy endeared him to those whom he came to be near in time of trouble. By an irony of fate, he who restored so many to health, till he was worshipped for what seemed a magical power of healing, could not, 'howso'er defended,' keep disease and death from his own flock. These 'severe afflictions' made him, always famed for a womanly softness of heart, all the more the beloved and trusted friend as well as the skilled physician. 'What am I to do?' asked a nigh distracted mother, seeing in the doctor's face she was to lose her child. 'You must give her back to the Lord,' he said, the tears pouring down his cheeks. 'My little Maggie was her age when He took her. I know what it is—how hard.'

He loved to be a bearer of good tidings. A lady came to him from abroad, said to be stricken with a fatal disease. Her mother, an old friend, brought her to consult him. He saw his patient, and then turned to her mother. She said he reminded her of St. Stephen, for she 'saw his face as it had been the face of an angel.' He spoke but a bare word, but the gladsome light on his countenance was to her the dawn of hope. He rang for his next patient. 'He is very abrupt,' said the invalid. 'Oh, my dear,' said her mother, 'you did not see the joy on his face; his own eyes welled with tears when mine filled with thankfulness.' To this same mother, when other doctors condemned her son, he gave hopes he might be spared a few years; and under Sir James's care he lived on, but his lease was nearing its close. The mother saw Sir James at a station, but with his quick, short steps he hurried to a cab. She overtook him, asking, 'Tell me, will my son die?' He replied in his silvery, soothing voice, 'Did I ever fail to face you when I had good news to give you?' She saw by his compassionate expression, his sad tone, her answer. 'Will I tell him?' she asked. 'Dear friend,' he said, taking her hand, 'your boy knows. Nature told him, as it has told you. You mutually held your peace, not to harrow one another. We doctors should leave such things for nature to tell. Her message somehow comes softly to patient and friends when there is no more hope of life here.' His patients early felt he had gone through deep waters, and he, having tasted of trials, was akin to them when they were grief-laden. Though he could sorrow with them, he could also build them up in courage.

The capability to laugh as well as to sympathise was a bond of union between him and children. He never passed a grandfather's clock with a child but 'rickory, dickory, dock' would bubble to his lips; and he would repeat the well-known lines in such graphic style, that the mouse running up the clock became nearly visible, and when it descended on the stroke of one, in hot haste he, with the eager listener, would hurry away. An old patient remembers the Professor watching her boy amusing himself playing cards, and with that leisure in the midst of urgent haste he seemed able to command, he sat down to 'catch the ten' with much avidity. As he left, he put his head in at the door to chaff and challenge his antagonist; and gave, as he hurried downstairs, a few pithy directions to the mother, for all the time he had been intent on the game, his face full of merriment, he had been thoroughly diagnosing his small patient. Casting back their memories to the days that are no more, many of these child-friends of his recall him. They all tell the same tale: 'Someone among the grown-ups we counted one of us;' 'Always so kind, taking trouble to making a lot of shy children unshy;' 'Always suggesting some new game or telling us some story;' 'Made us take up botany by interesting us about plants,' etc.

A daughter of his friend Robert Chambers recalled lately the first time she met him, when, someone failing to come for dinner, she was sent for from the schoolroom. A note also came at the last moment to say Professor Simpson was not to be waited for, and Miss Chambers found herself by a vacant chair; but the tardy Professor appeared soon, and, with his usual quietness of tread, slipped into the empty seat. His host wanted to move him to a more distinguished vicinity, but he stuck by his youthful neighbour. He found out all her tastes, set her athirst to study various branches he told her of, and what between seriousness and laughter, they began a lifelong friendship. She married, and came back to Edinburgh with twins. On taking her boys to show them to her friend, 'One in eighty,' he at once said, 'is the ratio in which the birth of twins occurs,' and ever after he wrote and spoke of her as 'One-in-eighty.'

He gave apt little nicknames to his young comrades. A little girl, 'a sole daughter,' had sat most staidly still while her mother and the Professor discussed at length some antiquarian find. He looked up and saw the well-behaved lassie sitting gravely, patiently by. 'Poor little Archæology!' he said, smiling at her, as he rose to look for a picture-paper for her; 'we must find something to interest you;' and he never ceased to call the quaintly quiet little damsel 'my little Archæology.' Another girl, very delicate, and burdened with the high-sounding name Augusta, and whom he recommended to be rubbed and fed on glycerine, he spoke of as 'Glycerina.'

When a very small child I had been left at Trinity with a nurse, when all the others had gone away, and my father often came down to the sea to sleep, out of sound of the door bell. He managed to write letters in my name during his rapid visits. I quote them to show how easily he descended into a four-year-old view of things. The first letter was refusing an invitation to a cousin's marriage, as 'I am at present so diligently engaged in the education of Chance, the dog (and a very bad dog he is sometimes), that I have not a day or even an hour to spare. Besides, the little money which I collected for the journey has been lately expended by me on the purchase of tin soldiers, for I am a promoter of this great Volunteer movement. By the bye, I've got a pair of "party" stockings, of which I am very proud, and a pair of new boots, which nurse wants to take off when I go to bed, but papa has told her I may keep them on —till I am asleep, he said.'

The next letter is a few years later, when I also had gone to that Isle 'with its green hills by the sea,' and my father writes, as usual, late one night in September: 'MY DEAREST EVE,—Of course there is no ink in that barbarous Isle of Man, or you would have written me long ere this. Try pencil—it will do quite well; and tell me what the first of womankind is doing, and how Mona's asthma is, for quadrupeds are necessarily far more interesting than bipeds, always (in Willie's estimation) excepting hens. All goes on here busily, as of old, especially from two to six. My new assistant, Dr. Aitken, has come. But I have got another very, very diligent assistant, who is ever extremely busy at work, except when he sleeps, and that occupation he indulges in rather deeply and long at times. His last occupation at night consists in carrying up to bed some thin book or other for him and me to study. Upstairs he marches most proudly with it in his mouth, bending his back and wagging his tail at such a furious and frantic rate that I sometimes fear for him, book and all, rolling backwards. He visits all the patients, but instead of feeling their pulses and asking them to put out their tongues, he smells at them and touches and licks their hands. Then, when he and I get back into the carriage, his first occupation generally consists of bolting up and trying to take my nose into his mouth. This, I fancy, is his way of asking "What kind of case is that which I have seen?" or of expressing his interest in the disease. But my paper is done, and I must stop. Love to Mamma and all. Ask Magnus what murders has he committed with his gun, and tell Willie I was greatly pleased with his letter. Puck sends his compliments to him.—Your affectionate papa, J. Y. S.'

His love for dogs developed when he became a householder, though his wife never shared his taste for them. Whenever he started his carriage and his two grey steeds, he got a Dalmatian to bear it company, called 'Glen.'

'Billy' succeeded him, and in an American doctor's journal, who visited him in 1855, he speaks of 'a Danish spotted coach-dog, a universal pet, which the Professor feeds as he eats his lunch and reads his letters.' We children all inherited his love for animals, and he and our dogs were firm allies, though Puck, the black and tan terrier mentioned in this letter, was his chief favourite. Other animals besides the canine members of his family received his notice and reciprocated it. He never passed a dog in a patient's house without a moment's halt to pat it or speak to it. It was certain on future visits to greet him with effusion. A parrot, which was given to his daughter Jessie, was long a delight to him. John Gray, it was called, but so many medical titles were afloat, it shortly called itself Dr. John Gray and Dr. Polly, and also degreed all the dogs. Jarvis taught it to hail its master by his new title, and Dr. John's 'Sir Chames,' said in a gentle voice, surprised and pleased his master. Dr. John lived in the dining-room window, and when 'Sir Chames' drove to the door, its flutter and whistle of delight forewarned the roomful waiting for him of his advent. A magpie belonging to a patient was fond of attracting his notice. It flew on to his head one day, and queried, in tones ludicrously like his, 'Well?'

My father's readiness to enter into the tastes of old folks or young, of duchess or fishwife, endeared him to all and sundry. His magnetic power of fascination, his exquisitely sympathetic manner, his divine gift of speech, are as difficult to portray by pen and ink as it was for an artist to catch the varied play of his expression. He may go down to posterity as one who fought against pain, as one who had a great gift of healing; but his power of inspiring, cheering, and loving his comrades and friends can only be known to those who knew the charm of his personality, the strong and tender love to his fellow-beings which dwelt within him. Spurgeon called him 'That dear angel of mercy, Sir James Simpson'; and added, 'If you knew ten thousand eloquent men in Scotland, I would give them work for the next hundred years, namely, to praise the Lord for sending to us such a man.' But, besides his expertness in dispelling sickness, Mr. Spurgeon had seen and felt the depth of lovingkindness that was in the Scots doctor.

Simpson earnestly preached to his students the necessity of not despising 'that gentle womanliness of heart which the sick in depression and pain so often look for, long for, and profit by. An unsympathising physician is bereft of one of the most potent agencies of treatment and cure. He knows not, and practises not, the whole extent of his art, when he recklessly neglects and eschews the marvellous influence of mind over body. For sometimes kindly and cheering words or looks from the physician are to the patient of more real worth than all his physic.' He was beloved by his patients, who had in them a most implicit faith in his skill, and all of whom personally adored him. It may be thought they exaggerated his good qualities, but those who were his contemporaries, who knew him as a fellow-worker, not their much-worshipped medical adviser, bear witness to the likeableness of his nature. 'But if no physician was ever more widely known, it is still more true that no man since the world was, was ever more greatly loved, and we do not exaggerate when we say that we never knew a *more lovable* man,' said the *Edinburgh Medical Journal* of him; and Professor Miller, in his Notes on Chloroform, writes of his sometime neighbour: 'We admire his talents, we praise his zeal, we rejoice in his success, and while we honour his genius, *we love the man.*' American physicians recognised in him not only an eminent and learned Scotch practitioner, but 'a philanthropist whose love encircled the world.' 'He was not too good for human nature's daily food, his goodness was never nauseating to ordinary palates,' said a journal of him a few years ago. At his house, as at another wise man's, 'all whom he knew met.' He could bring antagonistic elements round his table, and, by the wonderful leaven of his presence, amalgamate them. He could sweeten even enemies into friendship. The quick eye which could diagnose disease could also diagnose a character. The shyest was 'easily great' with this loved and honoured associate. He never spoke a few words to anyone but they were brighter and better for it. Dull faces even now light up as they recall to their memory his encouraging smile, his soul-reading glance. He could heal wounds by no mere skill of surgery, he carried a balm in his words. His blithe, silvery-toned voice, the lightsomeness he brought in with him, an old patient lately said, did her more good than any medicines ever invented. His talisman of attraction lay in the sincerity and simplicity of his life, and the cheerfulness, the tact, which comes from a good heart.

Simpson was the most benevolent of men, but he gave 'himself' as well as his gold. He climbed ungrudgingly up long stairs in the Old Town to visit the sick, and 'Very many of us,' records one of his professional brethren, 'have grateful occasion to recollect his devoted and unwearied attention to ourselves and our families in times of suffering, and none of us can ever forget the pleasant smile and the kindly grasp wherewith he was wont to greet us.' He gave freely of the draught of simple human pity which George Eliot held to be 'more helpful than all wisdom.' Many a man to-day remembers, when he stood on the threshold of life, how the Professor, when they had gone to take farewell of him, would follow him to the door and apologetically ask if he had enough 'filthy lucre' in his pockets to go out with into life. Nay, he would remark to them that it would be a favour to call upon him for a loan if need be; 'for I was poor too,' he said, 'and if my brothers hadn't helped me without stint, I would not be where I am to-day.'

He had unconventional but effective ways of compassing what he wanted. He jumped over small obstacles with the utmost calmness—obstacles that other people would have regarded as insuperable. He had always a readiness in him to meet difficulties which helped him in his profession. A bottle of chloroform which an assistant had upset on the floor, ran the supply short when it was most needful. Others looked blank or flustered. He cut out the square of drugged carpet, and thus kept the patient under the influence of the anæsthetic. He had resourceful ways of using whatever tool came readiest to hand. He found a ten-pound note was none the worse for being used as an effective pad to remedy a rattling window. He would roll an arrow-head or a piece of antique gold in a bank-note representing much wealth, and it insured Jarvis not mislaying his antiquarian find when he emptied his pockets. His methods were sometimes neither conventional nor tidy, but they compassed the object in view.

This was the man who, by the middle of this century, stout of heart and of good courage, with a mind seething with the fervour of invention, had scaled the heights of the cliffs of fame, and was yet athirst for more conquests over disease.

CHAPTER VI

SQUABBLES—HONOURS

'He who wishes to secure the good of others, has already secured his own.'—CONFUCIUS.

BEFORE 1850, Simpson had decided that the great wen of London would not suck him in, and that the field of his labours should be in the pleasant place in which his lines had been cast. There had been an attempt in 1848 to wile him up to London, but he found ample scope for work in Edinburgh, for patients sought him there in such numbers that he had, as a contemporary then said, 'crowded into every year three times as much research as a very industrious man could manage, ten times as much controversy, and twice as much practice.' He had a hearty love for the city wherein the greater part of his life was spent. He found, like Alexander Smith, that 'Residence in Edinburgh is an education in itself. It is perennial, like a play of Shakespeare's. Nothing can stale its infinite variety.' His antiquarian tastes had full scope within its bounds, his love for the beautiful had its fill, and he was proud in summer, when visitors thronged to it, to show them all its byways of history, the long grey hog's-back ridge of the Old Town from the Castle to Holyrood, and the Lion hill that watched over all, 'with the city's towers and gables anchored at its feet.' In Hans Andersen's Life it is mentioned, speaking of his visit to Edinburgh: 'The famous physician, James Simpson, was his *cicerone* through the town, and at Simpson's house he was frequently entertained, and there introduced to the leading notabilities of Modern Athens.' Besides delighting in 'Auld Reekie,' Professor Simpson knew he would sadly miss, if away from it, the chance he had every now and then to rush out to Bathgate, and rest for a few hours among familiar faces.

He had a goodly band of fellow-professors to associate with or joust with. He loved a foeman worthy of his steel, and he found both friend and foe in his Alma Mater.

Chloroform's success secured and prejudice worsted in the stern fight that threatened to strangle it at its birth, he still unceasingly wrought on, trying to discover further means whereby to mitigate pain and lay his finger on the source of sickness. He added many improvements to his own special line. Speaking of the advances he made in obstetrics, the *Daily Review* said comprehensively: 'Comparing the subject as Simpson found it with what it became after he had worked at it, is like comparing a block of rough-hewn marble with the almost completely chiselled statue. The simplicity of his methods of treating intractable diseases, the grand and sweeping generalisations at which his keen and rapid intellect would unexpectedly arrive, the persevering manner in which he strove to grope his way to new physiological or pathological laws, if he found existing ones too narrow to admit of his ideas, are examples of the conscientious, careful, and profound, yet simple and faithful way in which one of the most indefatigable and successful workers of the nineteenth century went about his great and arduous work. His are among the few modern works which are comparable to those of Hunter and the old masters of the art who lived and flourished in times long gone by, in the days when men put both body and soul, and life itself, into their books.'

'The medical practitioner can never cease to be the medical student,' he said; and, practising his precept, he searched diligently for more knowledge till the end of his days. In 1850 he revised and enlarged his papers on Leper Houses. Just a year before his death, he asked a friend visiting Norway to make further inquiries there on leprosy, as he had some theory that, unless guarded against, it might again prove a scourge. His research after this foul disease brought to light many forgotten statutes which had been in vogue to stop its ravages. These mediæval provisions for eradicating contagious disease by isolation suggested to him that the law in this century could rid us of preventible disease, a subject which much engrossed him later. Mesmerism and homœopathy were fruitful grounds for warfare in the beginning of the fifties, and he was, as usual, in the thick of the fight. He was censured in the *Lancet* for dabbling in *séances*, but he explained he had been trying to give them a fair trial. He offered in a letter to the Medico-Chirurgical Society to place five lines of Shakespeare in sealed boxes in their charge, and pay £500 to any clairvoyant who could read them.

Homœopathy was the cause of a long warfare. The *Lancet* had been twitting Edinburgh University with allowing one of its professors to practise its principles, and finally the authorities were obliged to reprimand the 'globulistic practitioner.' Professor Simpson had been presented with a tasteful box of homœopathic medicines, and had such implicit faith in their innocuousness that he presented it to his eldest son. Master David played peacefully for many hours with this new plaything, and, when still in holland blouses, having fixed on medicine as his future career, this toy had a real smack about it which he much relished. He emptied out its contents and refilled the phials as his fancy suggested. A doctor came in one day, captured the case, practised with it, and recounted the wonderful cures it had effected. Professor Simpson laughed merrily when he remembered seeing his son endlessly mixing its contents, and tried to joke his friend out of his newly confirmed theories. It was in 1851 that the war which had been smouldering long against homœopathy broke out in Edinburgh. Professor Simpson, believing it to be unscientific, and seeing too the charm its tenets were likely to have for nervous, fanciful people, with his usual promptness resolved to do his part thoroughly in the skirmish. The pamphlet elucidative of his views grew into a volume of some three hundred pages. No sooner was he finished with 'the last Edinburgh quarrel,' as this globulistic combat was called, than he took up the pen to fight *for* Professor Syme, long his avowed enemy. At some medical association at Oxford his brother professor had been censured, and with his usual Quixotic chivalry and love of truth, Simpson fought for Syme, affording thereby a fine example of a forgiving temper.

Death in these years had devasted the ranks of the

friends of his youth. Dr. John Reid, after much suffering, died. Misunderstanding separated him from another more recent comrade—a separation which sorely grieved him. His brother John, who had been so liberal to him, died in 1841. Another brother shortly after followed Mary across the seas, and they never met again. New members of the family and new friends were springing up. Edward Forbes's election to the Edinburgh Chair of Natural History was a counterbalancing circumstance, but he did not long live after his appointment.

Honours, meantime, came in thick upon him. Canon Farrar, speaking in Westminster Abbey of 'the priceless boon which God had granted to this generation in the diminution of pain,' mentioned that 'Of the discoverers —mainly four—it is a lesson not without its religious significance, that one alone had earthly rewards—that one whose bust is in this Abbey. Of the other three, two—such are earth's rewards if we work for them alone—died, after years of worry and disappointment, insane, and that by their own hand, leaving their families in poverty; the third, without wealth or honours, is living in an asylum now.' Perhaps, because he did not seek for renown, but had acted as in duty bound to do his utmost for his fellow-beings, he, on whose bust in the Abbey it is recorded, 'to whose genius and benevolence the world owes the blessings derived from the use of chloroform for the relief of suffering,' had honour paid him. In 1853, Dubois wrote to his *tres honoré confrère* that he had been made an Associate of the Imperial Academy of Medicine, Paris. He was elected with unique laurels. The members found that his name was not among those nominated, and a tumult arose. Shouts of 'Simpson—

Simpson!' began to be heard. The authorities were in a dilemma. Such rebellion was against the decrees of the commission; in fact, was entirely without precedent. Finally, however, his election was carried with unparalleled enthusiasm. 'The speeches,' said a newspaper of the time, 'made on the occasion gave rise to a display of wit which reflects honour on both parties;' while the President himself declared that 'although it had hitherto been considered that the greatest honour which the Académie could confer upon a foreign colleague was that of electing him amongst its members, yet it had remained for Dr. Simpson to prove that a greater honour yet existed, *that of being chosen in spite of the will of the Académie itself.*' He received the order of St. Olaf from the King of Sweden, and ere long was elected a member of nearly every medical society at home and abroad, besides being president of several. In 1856 he received from the French Academy of Sciences the Monthyon Prize for 'most important benefits done to humanity.' The detailed list of his honours would fill pages. No amount of flattery, praise, or earthly rewards effaced a bashful modesty inborn in him. When fame and honours were showered on him, he took them smilingly, for they would please those he loved dearest. Though praise gratified him, it left him still thoroughly humble of heart.

In answer to impromptu congratulations offered to him at a public meeting, after he had received his title, he truthfully said: 'The very cordial ratification of the step by all classes of my fellow-citizens has also added greatly to its value in my eyes. Then I have an elder brother who has ever been a father to me, who is a hundredfold prouder of the distinction than I am myself, and I confess that one of my principal pleasures in it has consisted in witnessing the deep and quiet joy it has given him.' Among other signs of fame in 1850, he was amused to find his name in Thackeray's *Pendennis*, and also that he was mentioned before that of a London contemporary.

In the fag end of his time he still kept himself abreast of current problems—schemes for better dwellings for workpeople, cottage convalescent homes, village flower shows to encourage gardening, that 'greatest refreshment to the spirits of man.' He gave substantial help to most of these projects. They all exist now seemingly as a matter of course, but then they were new ideas, and consequently looked at askance. Things scientific, too, received that wondrous 'orra moment' attention of his, during which he wrought so much for the public weal. Before the days of Mr. Darwin's *Animals under Domestication*, he had able people collecting information for him on the subject. Besides these enrolled allies, he gleaned knowledge from men of science, or from rustics who tended the beasts of the fields. Travelling constantly while engaged in his work of healing, he came into contact with all sorts and conditions of men, and he had a happy power of kindling an interest in others in whatever subject he was giving his mind to. High and low used their brains to help the Professor they loved.

He was interested in all old odds and ends,—'auld nick-nacket' things, and he amassed a motley collection, from a golden torc found in an Irish bog, or a ring of Queen Mary's from an East Lothian castle, to querns and arrow-heads from country ministers and doctors, who took to looking for antiquarian finds when they knew for whom the curiosities were intended. The amount of presents he received from 'grateful patients' filled his house with pictures, curios, and silver plate. His table was supplied with game, fruit, and flowers from wealthy friends; eggs, poultry, cheese, and scones from the humbler country folk.

His own alert observation often started him off into quite new ground. Observing that the men in some tweed factories were more than ordinarily robust, he learned they had an immunity from chest complaints and skin diseases, which he believed to be due to their working with oily wool and absorbing so much oil through their skins. He wrote on the subject to a medical paper, in 1853, and Mr. Robert Chambers drew attention to 'Oil Anointing' in his own Journal. Professor Simpson believed that the practice might help, if systematically prosecuted, to combat pulmonary diseases and scrofula. The sight of a Greek vase in the British Museum with a medical stamp and lettering on it, suggested to him an antiquarian hunt, to try and elicit more facts in regard to the cunning drugs the ancients used. This gave him the idea for the pamphlets, *Notes on some Ancient Greek Vases*, and *On Ancient Medicine Stamps and Medical Officers in the Roman Army*, all these entailing an enormous amount of study and investigation, for he never examined anything superficially. These samples show the varied range of the matters he took up, and how quick his mind was to apply stray suggestions to practical uses. He even in his lectures foretells the recent discovery of the Röntgen rays, thirty-five years before it occurred.

The years between '50 and '56 were therefore fully occupied, by the great increase of his practice and professorial duties, and by the numerous controversies connected with his medical and antiquarian researches. Every odd moment was used to add to his fund of information. But one thing he lacked time to do, and that was—to take rest!

CHAPTER VII

HOLIDAYS

'Cultivate not only the cornfields of your mind, but the pleasure grounds also.'—WHATELY.

HE had no broad margin to his life of leisurely thought. The pages of his day's work were printed to the very edge. His castles in the air were planned and foundations put under them as he travelled, waited at junctions, or sat by sick-beds in palaces or hovels. A patient watched his pen toiling through the night at a manuscript, and stretched out her hand impatiently and seized the aggressively busy pen, and bade him stop, which he did with that pliant amiability which came readily to him, and sat instead and read by the firelight, as he 'could not afford to be idle,' he said. Sir William Ferguson in 1848 strongly urged his contemporary to 'adopt the plan of getting away from business altogether for a month or so each year,' but it was advice he unfortunately did not follow. He was seldom off duty during the whole of the thirty-eight years he was an M.D. In vain he longed 'to get somewhere without a patient at the end of it.' Even escape from the sound of the never-silent door bell at No. 52 was a relief, and consequently a house at Trinity was an early realised dream of his. 'The shores of Forth,' he said in a letter, 'are most beautiful and soothing.' But he never had long for pleasant dalliance by them. No primrose path came into his walk in life. He fixed his abode at Viewbank, a square small house overlooking the sea and the sunsets, with some secluded space around it. Its ground was laid down in turf. He liked greenery to rest his eyes on, when he escaped of a summer evening from the grey city. Roses grew up the house in abundance. He planted laburnum, lilac, and apple trees in groups in the grass, and trees of white roses also stood side by side with the vivacious lilac. The cottage was simply appointed for a summer nursery, and not large enough to allow the too-hospitable owner to burden it with guests. It was a great relaxation to him. He bolted down the few miles which lay between it and No. 52 as often as he could. He could not idle even for a few hours. A load of books always came in the carriage with him. Another interest at Viewbank were his neighbours, the fisher-folk at Newhaven. He liked their independent ways and shrewd sayings. They liked his genuine simplicity and his ready help. He knew the sturdy breadwinners who sold the 'halesome faring' of the sea had no time for imaginary megrims. If they sent for him, it would need all his skill to save them from death. He always willingly attended them, and many a blue-petticoated wife, carrying her creel gallantly, has watched his carriage fly by, and stopped to audibly bless him for having restored her to health.

The fish dinners for which Newhaven is famous were a boon in an emergency to those who kept house at Viewbank. The Professor was a plain liver himself;

'tea, an egg, and a sunset' were his refreshments at Trinity; but he ofttimes arrived with some dozen distinguished foreigners on the plainly provided house. Usually Jarvis, his faithful servant, would follow him with the viands he had had ready at No. 52. While it was being prepared, the Professor would start his friends on a game of bowls, or sit by his favourite west window, looking up to the Highland hills.

Viewbank was but a tiny oasis, a brief few hours' rest in an endless stretch of work. A run to Bathgate he often mentions in letters as a red-letter day, but his farther afield holidays were murderously few.

Britons are said to take their pleasure sadly. He took his too busily. When he journeyed to foreign lands, his mind, full of varied interest, never rested. He hunted so incessantly and insatiably for knowledge, that those who accompanied him on his holidays remember them as a time of both mental and bodily overwork. When he went to Oxford to have his D.C.L. degree conferred, he accomplished so much sight-seeing that his companions were left breathless. 'Scampers,' he called them, and scampers at racing speed they were. Sometimes medical work took him scampering to Paris. His lack of French sadly annoyed him. He could converse in Latin, but many were not so glib at this dead language as he. He spoke French with so faulty an accent as to be incomprehensible, and the slowness of an interpreter impeded him. His ideas came rapidly, and his tutored eye saw so much he wished explained. My mother, in a letter to her sister, mentions: 'Yesterday, a Doctor Grumser came. He is Professor of Midwifery in Dresden, and has learned English on purpose that he may be able to talk with *our* Doctor.' The Edinburgh Professor wished he could have mastered foreign tongues to have had return chats. He introduced himself to a *savant* in Paris, who was profuse in his offers to do him honour, and at the end of a long list of proposed festivities, to prove his willingness and humbleness to do anything to please the Scotsman, he added, 'I will brush your coat for you myself.' 'I can tell you,' said my brother, who was there, 'he needed a brushing, but he wouldn't stop to let me do it, he was so keen on these hospitals. He never even took off the black tie he travelled in, though I offered to get him a white choker out of his portmanteau. He went all day in a dusty coat, from college to hospital, from hospital to museum, and got quite impatient because we could not ask questions quick enough for him.' 'We scampered over Switzerland in six days,' he writes to his wife. 'At Zürich Dr. K. was greatly amused at finding I was a doctor, as well as a pseudo-archæologist. He had been reading a paper on chloroform, and it suddenly struck him my name was connected with it.' Another time a Heidelberg doctor realised the man who had visited his ward, whose presence had struck him, was Simpson of Edinburgh, and embraced him, exclaiming, 'I always fancied Dr. Simpson was tall and old.' 'Est-il possible?' he kept asking, and finally, on parting, he beslobbered the Scotsman's cheek with kisses.

In 1851 he had a few weeks' foreign holiday to recover from a severe illness, brought on by blood-poisoning. On that occasion he asked Professor Syme to operate on his hand, though another able surgeon was his intimate friend; but he wished Syme to understand that, though they had disagreed, he had such a belief and trust in him as a man and a surgeon, that he would put himself under his care. Rome and Florence he visited in 1868, taking then, as his health was sorely failing, a longer scamper than usual, in company with his comrade, the late Sir John Pender. Many friends in the City of the Cæsars hailed his coming, and fêted him royally. They had a list made out of all the places he should see, and he accomplished all, and more, for his speed of action and the curious extent of his knowledge left many marvelling. He demanded to be taken to some sight his guides knew not of, but his tenacious memory had not played him false, though it might be something he had read of 'lang syne.' He hunted out the graves of Keats and John Bell (the surgeon-anatomist and author) in that Italian cemetery of which Shelley had said, 'It would make one in love with death to be buried in so sweet a place.' He had them trimmed and tended, and a rose which bloomed on Keats' grave after this was sent him. The *Scotsman* correspondent, speaking of this trip, said: 'Sir James's time has been much occupied in visiting the mighty ruins of the kings, republic, and emperors, the antiquities generally, hospitals, sanitary arrangements, and many other things of ancient and modern Rome, which claim attention from a mind like his, so full of knowledge, inquiry, and Christian philanthropy. His short period of recreation here has not been free from professional consultations, and a few even of the Roman nobility have anxiously solicited his advice; nor have any been sent empty away, for to one and all he has acted the part of the Good Samaritan. If time had permitted [he was but a week there], a public reception would have been given him.' That Roman trip was his last real holiday. Even his Continental scampers were matters of a fortnight's duration.

Occasionally he was lured in August over to the Isle of Man, where his hostages to fortune had preceded him. Its prescribed space held him at bay. It was in these days a secluded spot, before it became the lungs of Liverpool, into which convenience and cheapness of communication have transformed it. His antiquarian fancy found scope there, and he much enjoyed unearthing an ancient canoe, tracing Roman remains, and digging where he thought the Danes and other sea-kings had made a camp or buried their dead. His old coachman was asked if he and his nags were going. 'Me going there?' replied the Jehu contemptuously, looking across to Inchkeith, lying like a bright spot in the Firth, and imagining Mona's kingdom its mate in size. 'What would I do there? Drive round and round, and never get my horses exercised?' His master drove round and over the island, before a railway ran on it, and to be out of hearing of an engine's whistle was no small boon to him.

Once the Professor went to Belgium for two weeks to visit Scotch friends, and purposely left no address with assistants or servants. His wife knew it, but various strange rumours about his 'disappearance' began to get afloat, while he quietly enjoyed the foreign watering-place, with its gay lightheartedness. But alas! he seldom could so completely disappear.

Ireland, though he mightily disliked the crossing, he also scampered to. In one of his letters he mentions bog-trotting after a picnic, with a Bishop, to see some ancient stones. 'To discover some of them the Bishop removed four feet of turf accumulated on the bare face of the sculptured rocks.' The Irish Bishop in his episcopal hat, and Sir James in his unmistakable headgear, ample of size, easy of fit, must have been a curious couple, studying

> 'Grey recumbent tombs of the dead, in desert places,
> Standing stones on the vacant, wine-red moor.'

Amid the 'eerie and awesome' associations of that lonely place, the two enthusiasts revelled!

Inchcolm was a spot near by Edinburgh he sometook a half-holiday on. The hermit-saint's cell attracted him more than the abbey, still in such good preservation, for the mile's belt of sea from the Fife shore had saved it from being harried. In 1856 he mentions the 'beautiful Irish chapel' he found being used as a pigstye, and the same year he writes, anent his vacation prospects: 'This year I have not had a single holiday, and scarcely expect one now. I write this from Viewbank, which is very pretty this afternoon. Wherever Jessie and I may go, I doubt if we will see any place so pretty as the Forth and its shores. One day last week I crossed from Burntisland with one of the Eastern heroes, and he declared the scenery of the Bosphorus to be a joke to the scenery of the Forth opposite Granton.'

An American physician in his journal mentions a trip he had taken with my father to Loch Lomond side, and how the hotelkeeper, finding Sir James in the house, at once, unrequested, put the best accommodation at his disposal, consulted him about his daughter, and 'Before leaving we called for our bills, but were informed there was no bill against us.' Another hotelkeeper in the Highlands, who had reason to be grateful to the Professor, always longed to entertain some of his family. Some of the Professor's sons, not wishing to trespass on the good man's hospitality, passed his door on a walking tour. They had not proceeded far when a carriage and pair pursued them, and the driver insisted on them returning (for they had been recognised), and the shy boys were fed and housed, and sped on their way, after being lectured on not stopping of their own free will.

Sometimes my father did take a brief outing without the usual invalid at the end of it, but his idea of a holiday was an active one. After seeing patients in a continuous stream for days, he said he felt tired, and must have a rest. It was summer, and very warm, and his son proposed escaping to Viewbank, to bask or lie idling on the turf. 'That is no rest,' said his father. 'Go down and get Eve, and we will take a scamper round the Lakes, and be back to-morrow night.' Sometimes in the autumn, when Puck and he were the only two members of the family at home, he often wrote and said, '52 has been like a hotel all summer.' He longed for a big scamper, but did not see his way to it. Sometimes he had 'a delightful day at Bathgate,' which rested him; or a couple of days at some lordly seat, where he was an adored guest, would be his only relaxation. 'I had three happy days at Abbotsford,' he writes one summer, 'where little Walter Michael Scott was born a fortnight ago. He is Sir Walter's *first* great-grandson. He is called Michael after the wizard "Michael Scott," being himself as yet a very, very wee wizard.' Three days even was a holiday difficult to obtain. 'I have never been out of harness for three years,' he says casually in another letter, 'and I must get a week or two free of the bell and sick folk.' This total neglect of vacations drew heavy drafts on his health ultimately. A London doctor, when sending him a book of his on a 'Holiday Tour,' says: 'I wish, for health's sake, it had sufficient attractions to draw you to *do likewise*, as I cannot but fear your inconceivable activity may in the end work out the cerebral quarry before its time.' Quicksilver seemed to flow in his veins, which would not let him be idle, and anyone who knew how he was sought after by those in health, as well as by those who were sick, how his house was besieged, how he was waited for and waylaid between his carriage and that ever-open door of No. 52, knew how impossible he felt it was to take a holiday. 'I wish I had been busier,' he said, on one of his last days on earth. Then he asked dubiously, 'I *have* done a little work, don't you think?' It is difficult to see how he could have done more in his fifty-eight years of life, for he had overtaken work which would have employed several ordinary men, as he toiled on in the night, and his too few holidays were occupied, instead of resting, in gratifying his quenchless thirst for the acquisition of knowledge.

CHAPTER VIII

ACUPRESSURE—HOSPITALITY—ATTRACTIVENESS

> 'The tidal waves of deeper souls
> Into our inmost being rolls,
> And lifts us unawares
> Out of all meaner cares.'
>
> LONGFELLOW.

THE Professor's next big venture after chloroform in 'boons to humanity' was Acupressure, which he perfected and introduced in 1859. 'It is the rage at 52 at present,' he wrote. It was an invention by which veins were pinned, and thereby the use of ligatures after amputations was rendered unnecessary, with the consequent danger of festering flesh. First he had tried wire for tying the arteries, and then used needles. 'Tut, a pin,' was the quotation from Justice Shallow he put on a pamphlet on this subject. 'The introduction of this method of restraining hæmorrhage would of itself have entitled Simpson to enrol his name beside those of the greatest surgeons who have ever lived,' wrote a contemporary. He had wrought long at this idea. He was sure it was, as he said, 'a great thought.' In regard to most things medical he had a prophetic eye, for in the fourth and last of the graduation addresses he gave the students, he foretold many things which people blandly smiled at as some of Simpson's chimeras. This prophecy in regard to Acupressure has not as yet been realised. 'I shall be quite content if Acupressure begins to be thought of about a quarter of a century hence,' he said; adding, 'The surgical mind is a very curious piece of metaphysics.' The antiseptic treatment years later swept away the foulness left by the ligature. It was effectually used in Aberdeen and adopted in foreign hospitals.

It raised a storm in Edinburgh. 'Skip your ain side, captain,' said one curler to the head of another rink, in reply to advice as to the most strategical way of placing the stones on a neighbouring rink. 'Skip your ain side,' said the surgeons in strong terms to Professor Simpson. 'Keep to obstetrics, and leave surgery to us;' but the said Professor was obdurate. He held his M.D. diploma, his power to wield the healing rod of Æsculapius qualified him to push on in any branch which eased suffering humanity, so a fierce war began between him and Professor Syme. In February 1865 the following notice appeared in an Edinburgh newspaper:—'It is often stated that when the notorious surgical teacher, Paracelsus, wished to show his aversion to any particular author, he immolated the writing he dissented from in the presence of his pupils. We are not aware that this mediæval practice has ever been adopted in any of our Scottish Universities till last week, when it was followed out in one of the classrooms of the University of Edinburgh. Mr. Syme took this pamphlet [Dr. Simpson's *Answer to Objections to Acupressure*] into his classroom, and without attempting to answer the rather unanswerable arguments which it contains in favour of

Acupressure, he scolded at the author, and declared the pamphlet to be a piece of "vulgar insolence." Then came the *dénouement*; with firm hand, teeth compressed, and altogether a most determined and savage expression, he tore the pamphlet in two, gave the fragments to his assistant to be consigned to the sawdust box with other surgical remains.' This raised further discussion in the medical papers and circles. The book Sir James wrote on Acupressure is a fat volume of nearly 600 pages, and is full of notes and statistics. The very warfare on its merits necessitated a heavy amount of literary work, sufficient to keep one man busy; but its originator was not one man, but many, so he managed to overtake the amount of penmanship it entailed, without interfering with his enormous practice.

By the time Acupressure, which was some ten years chloroform's junior, was given to the world, the originator of them had become a man of very great note. Every year since he had been made a professor had brought him more renown, and consequently more practice, and more friends to trespass on his time. His patients came from the uttermost parts of the earth,—from Iceland or some Pacific isle, from Darkest Africa or the Great Lone Land. The Siamese Twins breakfasted with him, and he advised them not to try and separate company. He longed for Röntgen rays (which he tried on them by a cursory method of his own), to see if he were right. Besides coming from every clime, his patients were of every rank. Whoever had most need of his skill was to him the chiefest. The veriest pauper could arrest his attention readier than 'a marquis, duke, and a' that,' if they had some peculiar malady.

He was unsparing in his attention to patients, not in order to lay up for himself riches here, but, as Tennyson said—

> 'Give to the poor,
> Ye give to God,
> He is with us in the poor.'

Sir James gave his brains without stint to those who asked him to diagnose their ailments or had need of his skill. He was preparing to allay sciatica, with which he was suffering one evening, by a steam bath. He suddenly called for his boots and dressed himself, and told his assistant he had forgotten to see a patient whom he had promised to visit. In vain the junior doctor begged of him not to risk a further chill, for the patient was in no extreme of danger. 'No,' he said firmly; 'I must go. I promised, and she will fret if I do not, or only send a substitute, and she has suffered so much.' Another old friend reminded me of a fact she knew of. A country doctor from some ten miles south of Edinburgh arrived late one night, demanding the Professor. Jarvis, who answered the night-bell, sternly refused to let his master, who had not been in bed for a week, be roused, but the doctor wrote on his card and insisted on the Professor seeing his appeal. As soon as the Professor had read it, he sent for the doctor, and while dressing issued orders for a fresh horse, and left with him. He overlooked the instruments the assistant had packed, stopped at the College, rung up the porter to get another from his classroom, and, despite the jolting of the carriage, slept. He saved a poor woman's life, whose case, except under his skill, was hopeless, and his country colleague landed him, after his gratis services, back at No. 52 in the grey chill dawn. He had slept the whole way back, the sleep of a wearied man, saying, 'It is the only visit to the Land of Nod I'll have a chance of for another twelve hours.' At a patient's one day he sat down on a low stool. 'Oh, Dr. Simpson, don't sit on such a lowly seat,' she said. He shook his head sadly. 'It is high enough for all I deserve, for your case has baffled me to diagnose'; and as to receiving a fee from her, for he attended her constantly, always hoping to get some clue to the malady, he declined any. 'I have done nothing, I deserve nothing,' he said. On the day he sat so humbly by her couch, he looked extra tired, and she asked why. 'Well,' he said, 'I'll tell you. I was in a room six stairs up in the High Street last night, trying to save a poor woman who had been brutally mauled by her husband. I happened to meet the police, and they asked me to look at her, and I think she'll live.' On another occasion he arrived, 'wat, wat, and weary,' at a rich patient's house on the outskirts of Edinburgh on a Sunday night, and explained his late arrival on foot. 'I stopped to see a woman in the Grassmarket who is very ill, and some of her neighbours told my cabman how "far ben" she was, and that they concluded I'd stay there. So did he, for he drove off, and it being Sunday, I could not get another cab. I will see her again on my way home—if I get home to-night.' This incident showed how confident 'the masses' (including the cabman) were that their renowned doctor would give his aid and deprive himself of sleep to relieve some poor inmate of a poverty-haunted district, and thus substract some particle from the great heap of human suffering.

But it was not only the sick that thronged to his house. For years his name, his versatility, his influence, attracted men, some full of an incomplete invention, others to show a discovery they were about to patent, authors of renown, authors with unpublished books, young hopefuls wanting advice or snubbing, men of science, art, and literature in Europe, who came north of the Tweed, wanting to meet this man of genius. Strangers from every continent sought him. He saw everyone that came, though sometimes it was just a glance or a word that he had the chance to give them; but he advised, loaned, cheered, and chatted with thousands. His wide survey of all matters, his own greed for knowledge, which made him as attentive a listener as he was a successful questioner, his ability to talk of medicine or grouse, of railways or politics, of history or poetry, assured him a welcome wherever he went, and, like a magnet, he drew people in crowds around him by the spell of his genius.

The amiable gentleness he had inherited from his mother had been a goodly endowment to him. His manners came from his heart, and it being true and steadfast, he was at ease in any company. Courtesy came to him naturally. No one could overawe him, for his self-reliance made him quietly hold his own. There was no false note about him, no fawning, no bragging, but an earnestness and kindliness which made him interest himself in everyone. He always had time for a word, or a message, or a smile for people, however insignificant. While storing his mind with treasures, he, at the same time, made all welcome to its purest ore. Even in his callow medical days he jotted down in his letters bits he thought would interest the folks at Bathgate, remarks on dress for Sandy's wife, or agriculture for his brother. 'Lady Lorne came down to dinner with a *most* beautiful chaplet of real heather round her braided hair. I think now artificial flowers very ungenteel,' he wrote to his sister-in-law from Erskine House. He noted dress with his Argus-eyes, which saw so much.

A paper as far back as 1855, describing a luncheon at No. 52, gives a vivid description of what went on daily for the ensuing fifteen years. 'In the season, assembled unceremoniously in a moderate-sized room, with nothing in common save their wish to meet their host, you find a company drawn together from every latitude and longitude, social and geographical. Of all this motley party who are chatting in momentary fellowship, and watching, with faces amused or anxious, the conversation of their more accessible neighbours, there is probably hardly one who is not in some way or other notable; but the grades and classes of eminence run through nearly the whole gamut of social distinction, from duchesses, poets, and earls, down to the author of the last successful book on cookery, the inventor of the oddest new patent, a Greek courtier, a Russian prince, or a German count. At your elbow the last survivor of some well-known shipwreck is telling his terrible story to the wife of that Northern Ambassador, who is meeting with the softest of the Scandinavian dialects the strong maritime Danish of the clever State Secretary opposite. At the table are three poets, half a dozen litterateurs, and as many celebrated doctors, some Americans. That mercurial gentleman with the small eyes and sharp face and Jeffrey-looking head, who is rattling away with such volubility and quicksilver action, is Professor Blackie. The tall Danton-faced man now speaking to Professor Hodgson is Aytoun. The sculptor is waiting to ask the opinion of the many-sided Professor which of these sketches should he do in marble. That quiet creature in black with the beautifully balanced head, who only listens, is an authoress of great promise. We are still learning the last price of provisions at Melbourne, from the Australians who have come from the land of gold in search of what gold cannot buy, when a carriage at full pace stops,—in a moment Dr. Simpson enters.

'With a few genial nods, shakes of the hand to the nearest, he begins to despatch the coffee and roll put ready for him, while a brother Professor at one ear propounds a question of University discipline, and a soldier just arrived from the seat of war [the Crimea] is giving him, at the other, the anecdote with which before evening the doctor will, in abrupt episode of consultation, have amused a hundred patients. In ten minutes the indefatigable Professor is again professional. Beckoning some patient, he disappears to the consulting-rooms, or news comes by telegraph that some poor peasant's wife, in some far village, is in the dangerous stage of some medically interesting calamity. There are none-knows-how-many wealthy invalids waiting their turn, but kind-heartedness and the delights of a desperate case prevail, and the doctor is off across the Forth, and will not be back till midnight.'

A friend from 'Brighter Britain' recalls the day when, as a small child, weeping copiously, she was dragged to No. 52 to be doctored, and sat sobbing by the recess of the dining-room window. She noted a brougham come to a sudden full stop at the kerb, saw the stir of expectancy among the guests, and she writes: 'I remember, distinctly as yesterday, a lane opened up among the people, and I saw a very *big little* man with flowing grey hair approaching. I loved him before he even spoke. His voice was very gentle, and he breathed rapidly, almost panted, while speaking. He sat down to lunch with a salver of letters and telegrams at his right hand. While he read and glanced at his letters, he talked to those round the table, introducing some, interesting all.' He suddenly espied his small patient, and, calling her to him, he said, looking at her hard, 'We'll soon stop St. Vitus's dance; meanwhile, I've a lassie just your age, Kitty.' He went out and shouted 'Jessie.' When his wee-est Jessie —his Sunbeam—came, he committed Kitty to her care. It was one of his happy introductions, for this began a sisterly friendship between the two girls, which survived across half the globe, and only death parted them. 'My next visit was as eagerly anticipated as the first had been dreaded, for I loved "52" a good deal better than my own home,' wrote Kitty, 'and knew every corner of it. Jessie and I used to go into the drawing-room and look at all the beautiful things, most of them the gifts of grateful patients, and always being added to. The furniture was all carved Indian work, given by someone. We used to be vexed when we found patients had overflowed from their *salon* there, and our prowl among the pretty things ceased.' They used to dust his books with their handkerchiefs, coax Jarvis to let them pour out his tea or run some errand for him. One small guest filled his cup to the brim with sugar, as she helped people to its sweet seasoning in proportion as she liked them, and she complained the big cup he used was not ample for her expression of love. Those who knew the house well, and had not had a word at lunch with him, lingered till his tea came up at four, and caught him then. It would have been interesting to know who all had sat round that selfsame table below which he had fallen in that first trance of chloroform, more like to death than its twin-brother sleep. Their names would form a portly volume, but all who met there remember how the leaven and lovingkindness of his presence cemented them together, even if of divers creeds, colours, and nations, with a firmly knit bond of union. He lifted his company from meaner cares, he illumined them by his intelligence, while he refreshed himself in their company, learning from them. 'When Simpson bustles in,' says a writer, describing a crowd of guests awaiting him at lunch, 'under the genial influence of his presence all tongues are set a-wagging; and well may you ask whether the men who leave his house after luncheon are those who but an hour ago regarded each other with cold disdain. For now they are cordial, kindly, sympathetic; each has been induced to show whatever was attractive in his nature, or to give the fruits of his experience.'

Many who came through that open door to sit by him through national reticence could not express their feelings of gratitude and goodwill towards him so prettily and feelingly as did a Swedish doctor, Magnus Retzius, who wrote: 'Would Almighty God that any occasion might present itself to me to show how much I am thankful for your kindness to me, dearest friend! My feelings come in agitation, and my eye becomes tearful whenever I think that I perhaps no more in this life will see the man to whom I am so much indebted, and to whom my heart finds itself so strongly stirred.'

CHAPTER IX

MONEY MATTERS—RELIGION—TITLE AND AFFLICTION

'Great souls are always loyally submissive, reverent to what is over them.'—CARLYLE.

'QUEEN STREET has been like a private hospital and hotel all summer,' he wrote one autumn when we were all away. It was often so. He followed the Great Physician's commands, 'I was sick and ye visited me,' and 'I was a stranger and ye took me in.' Sir James always found a brother to minister to. He had a room below that wherein his wealthy patients waited, for those who were poor and needy; they were attended to by his assistants, and when any peculiar or difficult case came to their notice, the Professor came down and gave his advice. An American physician who was a guest at 52 Queen Street says: 'He goes through this great labour quietly, methodically, with as gentle, kindly a spirit as ever man manifested. The moral character of the daily service in disease is quite as striking as is the professional. The moral presides over the whole, and renders it one of the most interesting matters for observation that can occur. I have been utterly surprised at its executive patience, its efficient activity. Here are poor and rich together, and I can say from a long and wide observation that there is no difference in their treatment. The great fact of each in Professor Simpson's regard is that disease exists, which it is the physician's business to investigate and try to remove. He had time for everything; it was so quiet, so thorough, that though time was pressing on new engagements, it seemed as if the present one only occupied his mind.' He was electrically rapid in his diagnoses. His eye seemed charged with Röntgen rays, able to penetrate through the obscuring veil of flesh, able to detect the menace of disease and stop its blight. A clergyman was resigning his charge because of ill-health, which no one seemed to understand. He consulted Sir James. 'I think,' he said, 'you have two diseases which are very rarely united, but I am not quite sure yet. The two diseases I think you have, are described here; read these pages, and I will return in half an hour;' and the Doctor dog-eared two pages and left his patient, who says: 'As I read, I realised all my symptoms were accurately described, and I felt my case was understood at last. A crushing burden was rolled off from my mind, and hope returned to me. His insight into my case seemed to me almost supernatural, and it was all gained in three or four minutes. He cured me within twelve months.'

The patients in the saloon drew lots for priority, and he saw them between lunch and dinner, a quick clapping of his hands, oftener than the bell, warning the maid who regulated the rotation to 'come away' with another. 'Come away' was a favourite expression of his. He was always craving to be up and doing, and had to rouse more dallying folk with his spurring 'Come away now.'

Only once did he ever find fault with a fee. He was to

attend a patient in the North of England. She had fidgeted for his presence much sooner than the appointed time, and with other engagements it was impossible for him to grant her request to come 'as a guest.' He was preparing to start on the day fixed when he received yet another telegram warning him, 'Don't come too late.' He arrived. The husband of his patient met him on the doorstep, telling him his services were not required. In the telegram he intended to convey the meaning not to come, as they had anticipated matters. The Professor would likely have gone quietly home and never remonstrated if no fee had followed him, but the rude brusqueness of the man's manner, his stingy wording of his telegram, put the Doctor's back up, and despite his easy-going, forbearing nature, there lay, not so very deep, a stubborn obstinacy. He insisted on seeing his patient, he insisted on his legitimate dues, and would have gone to law to vindicate his claim. There is on record a striking example of how willingly he gave advice free of all thought of wealth as reward, and also of his honesty of purpose by not encouraging those who had no need for his potent skill to spend their money on fees and waste his time. He had a call to Brighton to see a lady whose illness was imaginary, who liked to boast of the sums she spent on doctors and specialists. He refused to go. His time was needed by those really ailing. In vain she wired to bribe him with the offer of a thousand pounds. Next week he heard Spurgeon's wife lay nigh unto death, and he offered his services and hurried South to save her. 'You will go on to Brighton?' suggested his assistant. 'The thousand-pounder still wires and writes, offering any sum if you'll go and see her.' 'No,' he said; 'it would be humbug. I told her she isn't ill, and she won't believe me. She'd better put some of her guineas into some struggling doctor's pockets. I need my time here to work.' He never took a fee from clergymen or their families. 'I'll wait till you are archbishops,' he said; 'meanwhile I'll take my fee in prayer, as the prayer of a righteous man availeth much.' Those who could well afford to pay, and trespassed on his consulting-hours, he often allowed to forget that his time was golden. Sometimes he received cheques of princely magnificence, sometimes they were strangely small for the depth of the purse they came out of. Jarvis, Clarke's successor, a quaint character, but honest as the day, emptied his master's pockets and gave their contents to my mother. Sometimes Jarvis, knowing the Professor's daily rounds, and also knowing the crowds of wealthy people he had admitted for consultation, would complain to his mistress that, judging by the contents of the Doctor's pouches, the labourer had not been regarded as worthy of his hire, or would conjecture who was likely to have borrowed from his master.

My father loved to give, though he was often chary of receiving. A man of money, but one who had been kind to one of his elder sons, sent a cheque for professional advice; but he sent it back, 'for you have done for mine more than I can repay'; and many a sum which came in his letters to him, he told his assistants to return, for he knew the senders could ill spare it. If expostulated with for taking too little from many who had money in plenty, he turned obstinate, or, shaking his head and smiling, said, 'I prefer to have my reward in the gratitude of my patients.'

This careless haphazardness in regard to money came only upon him when he had earned 'bread and fame'—two things, he said in 1868, he had come to Edinburgh forty years before to fight for, and won. When he was a student living on his family's savings, he kept a most rigorously exact account of his expenditure.

One of the unbusiness traits in his character frequently was complained of. He never kept a list of the patients he had to see; he relied on his memory, which never forgot a really urgent case; but imaginary ailments or megrims—a terrible disease, he said—he left unattended or forgot when other work overwhelmed him. He was deluged with angry expostulations from these neglected ones; but once he and his patients met, the glamour of his manner disarmed their displeasure. 'I'll see you in Princes Street,' he said to a hypochondriac who asked when they would meet again. 'Take a walk there daily in the sun; that is all I can prescribe.' She was most indignant at his hard-heartedness, but finally tried his cure.

Again, his patients, by want of thought, not only troubled him and wasted what he was more careful of than money, namely, his time. He would receive a letter asking him to call at 'their hotel,' and he would spend precious minutes trying to find which hotel. 'I'll get a terrible blowing up all the same,' he said, 'though I asked for them at several.' 'Why was not our cheque acknowledged?' writes an indignant person—the reason being, no address was sent! 'Send me some more of that white powder you gave me. It was in a big wide-mouthed bottle, and you emptied it on to a sheet of paper. That was two years ago,' writes another, never indicating what the white powder was intended to cure. These are but a few samples of many complaints which poured in on the Professor—midge-bite annoyances which fidgeted him. He disliked giving offence, as heartily as he disliked seeing anyone's feelings wounded. He would sometimes dart a scathing glance from out of his deepest eyes, when an uppish assistant, with an air of superiority, smiled at some homely guest's homely manners. He found an able lieutenant in his wife, who helped him to put all at their ease, and to reassure some shy, diffident stranger that he was welcome.

Through some weekly newspapers, religious booklets, and biographies, a wrong impression as regards Sir James's religious character has been spread abroad. They have fostered the idea that before he was caught in the waves of a revival tide early in the sixties and 'converted,' as they put it, he had been an unhappy, unthinking, godless man, careless of the Hereafter, living solely in the present, and that only when under this new influence did he achieve any renown. His life's work lay behind him by then, short in years, but like to one of whose early death he himself spoke : ' He was older than some of us who are twice his age.' One has but to look into Sir James's daily life, into his letters, to see he had throughout his career, from start to finish, an all-simple but all-sufficient faith.

In 1842, when addressing the students (and being absolutely free from cant, he was not given to speak but what he believed himself), he said: 'May God in His infinite goodness enable you to select the better path, and may you ever be found asking for and relying upon the arm of His Omnipotence as the only sure and steady guide of your footsteps through it, so that when the journey of life is drawing to its close, you may have it in your power to look backwards upon time without remorse, and forwards upon eternity without fear.' This was advice which as a man of thirty-one he gave publicly to his newly-budded fellow-doctors, and is one example how full his thoughts were of the Great Physician. All his life he had been a God-fearing and God-loving man. He learned from his prayerful, devout mother to put his trust implicitly on High. 'He was a man,' as a writer in a weekly journal recently said of him, 'who never had stood shuddering on the brink of either the sea of life or the eternal future. *Act and trust* were his mottos. He did not stay to ask, "Can I swim?" Sinking or swimming, weary or refreshed, he struck out for the shore, trusting God with a whole heart.' His forebears had been superstitiously pious, with a chronic dread hanging over them of a stronger Power which had to be conciliated. Sir James's piety had reverence but no fear in it. He had perfect reliance and belief in Divine mercy and love, and this had been implanted in him as a child and grown up with him. The words 'God is Love' were inscribed on a watch a patient gave him. 'Your selected text,' he wrote, 'will, I trust, enable me to speak words of strength whenever I stand by the bedside of a dying patient—strength to her in her weakness, and words of life to her in the hour of her bodily death.' His profession led him to witness many a death-scene, and he was often called on to 'smooth the stormy passage to the grave.' He never became hardened to sadness and pain, for the deep compassion in his heart ever welled up to his lips and eyes when he saw others in physical or mental distress. He soon learned that the belief in 'the sure and certain hope of a blessed resurrection' sustained those who 'walked in death's dark vale,' and was an unfailing 'rod and staff' to comfort those who had to lose their loved ones. He was no theologian. His faith had come to him as if inborn. He never had to think out his belief. He had always *felt* it. Speaking to his nephew Robert (his Sandy's youngest boy), he said, 'I have unshaken confidence in Jesus only. I have mixed a good deal with men of all shades of opinion. I have heard men of science and philosophy raise doubts and objections to the gospel of Christianity, but I never for one moment had a doubt myself.' He was one who

> 'His god
> He cabins not in creeds;
> And in the hearts of men he finds what no man finds in books.'

The simplicity of his nature, despite his deeply thoughtful mind and his argumentative abilities, led him to believe in the gospel with the perfect, unquestioning belief of a child. He knew his Bible from cover to cover. It was his companion throughout life. A guest described what the Professor called 'his study.' Taking hold of a movable gas-burner, he brought it forward so that he could easily read on his pillow. 'Here,' said he, 'is my study. Here I read at night;' and among the divers changing volumes which littered his bedroom, there was always close at hand 'The Buik' which he had learned to read standing at his father's knee.

Professor Simpson joined the Free Church movement in 1843, and was of the body that marched down to Tanfield. His face is among the group painted by Mr. D. O. Hill to commemorate that great event. His Huguenot blood rebelled at what he believed to be religious oppression; but at the same time, rigidly truthful, he refused to become an elder of the Church, because of certain doctrines in the Confession of Faith with which he did not agree. He sat under Dr. Guthrie whenever he could get to church. He used to glide up the aisle with that firm, yet silent step of his, and people, looking round after a prayer, would start to find that, though late, he had so quietly taken his seat among them. Dr. Guthrie and he were firm friends. 'We had a minister yesterday,' he complained, 'a good man, but his sermon was wersh, wersh, and, oh, cauld, cauld! Why *will* not men speak as if they believed what they said, and wished others to believe it? Just look at Guthrie—what zeal and fire!' Like Longfellow, he could say: 'To me a sermon is no sermon in which I cannot hear the heart throb.'

In 1862 a domestic affliction heavily smote the Queen Street household. 'Our Jamie died most calmly and peacefully, just before the church bells began to ring,' my father wrote to Bathgate. This Jamie was the third son and namesake, and, like his sister Jessie, they seemed born with heaven's stamp upon them, and exempt from the failings and tempers so prevalent in others. They bore ill health and suffering without a murmur; they soothed those around by their brightness and unselfishness. Writing of Jamie, his father said: 'My assistant, Dr. Berryman, and he were great companions. He taught him latterly turning and carpentering, for, though half blind, he worked away wonderfully by touch, making boxes, desks, cages, etc., for his little brothers and sisters. He had the garret room over my bedroom fitted up as a workshop, and as I was laid up lately with this sore throat, the knock of his busy little hammer and the birr of his turning-lathe were, somehow, pleasant sounds. They are all silent and still there now, and I listen for them in vain.' The boy's helplessness, his long period of suffering, had specially endeared him to his parents, who had lavished extra care upon their stricken son.

Professor Simpson was an emotional man. He had not inherited from his ancestors their shrewd thriftiness in regard to money, but his veins had more than their full share of the warm French blood which made him, for a Northerner, strikingly impressionable, and occasionally guided by impulse rather than by calculation. This name-son's death, worked as a handle by others, made him deem it his duty to take a public part in revival work. 'We must all speak for Jesus,' the dying boy had said; and so his father, whose persuasive eloquence made him a noted lecturer, for a while spoke publicly on sacred matters. He quietly dropped this public testimony, on seeing among those with whom he had to associate, the profession without the practice, which it was impossible for him to favour. As a medical contemporary truly said of him: 'As a Christian, we believe him to have been a humble follower of his Lord.' This phase of his character is, however, too sacred to be enlarged on, and would not have been alluded to but for a mistaken part which his impulsive nature led him to play. Simpson was too true a man not soon to discover that the faithful discharge of duty for Jesus' sake was for him as noble a proof of his love to Him, and as certain a means of doing good to his fellow-men, as preaching and praying in public, however eloquently or impressively these services might have been performed by him. Among his medical *confrères* who did not know his simple sincerity of nature, this public profession of religion was looked on as a piece of eccentric cant, at which they shrugged their shoulders, and used as a handle to belittle him. But Sir James was no humbug, or one to do things merely to court attention.

'What do you consider was the greatest discovery you ever made?' an interviewer asked of him. 'That I have a Saviour,' replied the Professor, without hesitation. It was a discovery, not, as many imagined, dating only from 1862, but one which he had early made, and consequently his span of years was surrounded by that 'peace of God which passeth all understanding.' His whole life also had been one long prayer, for he had ever believed in the Benedictine injunction, *Laborare est orare*. If to work is to pray, no monk giving his life up to devotion had more earnestly prayed without ceasing than did James Young Simpson.

It was a sad irony of fate that he who healed so many could not ward pain and death from his own fold. His first-born, his sweet-souled little Maggie, at four years died in agony, begging for water which her closed throat would not let her swallow. Another daughter, a 'Mary,' had but a year's lease of life. Jamie had from infancy been a sufferer, and the darkness of blindness was closing in on him when he was lulled to rest 'by the sure enwinding arms of cool, enfolding death.' His sister Jessie, whom her father had early christened 'Sunbeam,' had been a special joy to him. He liked Jessie to 'tease' him as he sat at his desk, and make him spare a few minutes for a romp with her. As she grew up, her father and she were close companions. A round robin had been sent from the Isle of Man begging that Jessie might remain longer. His reply is before me now: 'To Miss Simpson, etc. etc. Ladies and Gentlemen, I will do myself the pleasure of answering duly your petition, provided that you send me one properly spelled and properly punctuated.—I have the honour to be, your obedt. servant, J. Y. S.' And after this sheet of chaff he put 'over,' and on the other side writes, 'By the bye, if any of you happen to see my darling daughter Jessie, be so good as to tell her that I have so much esteem for her good sense that I, as her physician, will allow her to remain or not, a week or so longer, just as her own wisdom and discretion dictate to her.' Her New Zealand friend lately recalled her recollection of Jessie the first time they met. It was still clear to her mind despite the lapse of years. 'An auburn-haired girl entered when your father shouted "Jessie." She had mild brown eyes, and a look of indescribable openness, gentleness, and courage combined.' Her doubtful health had given him much anxiety, but he was hopeful she might outgrow it. His eldest son, David, was devoted to his sister too. David came home from foreign studies in 1865, a well-trained M.D., brilliant, popular, full of health, and anxious to take the brunt of work from off his father's overloaded shoulders. He began his duties as assistant with tactful energy. He saw with practical perception how his father's unbusinesslike qualities led to greater demands on his time than necessary, how his goodness of heart let him be harassed by those whose thoughtlessness trespassed on his precious moments. Dr. David set himself gradually to free the house of those who clogged the wheels of work, and to alter some lax ways which would save his father fatigue, and give him time to devote to those whose severe or unique illnesses specially demanded his skill. The Professor found his son welcomed because he was his son. Patients grumbled if the assistant came, but when the assistant proved to be Dr. Davie, with the voice so like his father's, and the same blending of cheerfulness and determination graven on his face, he was accepted as a substitute. He thus found his buoyant-spirited and popular son lightened his duties. On the New Year's Day of 1866 the Professor was offered a baronetcy, the first physician practising in Scotland to whom that title had been granted, and great were the rejoicings in Edinburgh at this honour. But on the heels of this mark of royal favour came a mandate from the King of kings, not to claim the gentle girl of seventeen, whom father and son had nursed and tended with such care and devotion, but the great Reaper 'took the bearded grain at a breath.' After a few days' illness the stalwart young doctor, who was fast becoming so useful a colleague to his father, died. In a few weeks more his sister, too frail to stand such a shock, quickly faded; so, while the year was still little more than a month old, Sir James had two crushing afflictions to face. He was a man of wide sympathies and a large heart. But his love for his fellow-creatures in general did not weaken his affection for his own kin, and any bereavement he felt with all the sensitive keenness natural to so sympathetic a spirit. The shroud which overwork had been weaving for him began to wrap itself more closely round him. Speaking of his eldest son when the dark shadow of death hung over his house, Sir James wrote: 'My darling little Jessie is greatly broken down by this catastrophe. I fear she will not long be with us. She is very helpless in bed, and would allow no one to dress her sores but Davie, "gentle Davie," as she declared no hand to be *so* soft and kindly as his. I never knew how very, very dear *he* was to my heart till now he is gone from us for ever, and I cannot tell you in words the kind and unceasing care with which he has latterly watched over me, to save me all possible trouble and anxiety in all possible ways.'

'I felt this baronetcy such a bauble in health,' he wrote, 'and now, when sick and heartsore, *what* a bauble it is!' The rejoicings which followed its conferring had been great. 'I have shaken hands daily for two or three days till my arm is weary,' he writes. 'And the proudest of all about this New Year's gift is your uncle at Bathgate. At all events, he is a thousand times prouder of it than I am. In fact, when it was first offered me, I was rather ashamed to speak of it, and doubted about accepting it. But it was decided at last otherwise. Twice before I have avoided being Sir'd, but this offer was made in such very kind and gracious terms that it was difficult to refuse.[1] It seems to have caused much

---

[1] The following is the letter:—

OSBORNE, 3*d January* 1866.

DEAR DR. SIMPSON,—Your professional merits, especially your introduction of chloroform, by which difficult operations in surgery

joy in Edinburgh and everywhere around, and everybody pokes at me their "Sir," which I would be glad to avoid.' 'All Edinburgh has been here,' said his wife. 'They seem prouder of the honour than he is.' The world rejoiced with him then as heartily as in a few weeks later it sympathised with him. The letters of condolence which followed on the heels of those of congratulation came from the uttermost parts of the earth, from castles and from cottages, from millionaires wishing their money could buy 'surcease from sorrow,' from tramps in the slums, possessing not even a penny stamp. There were letters, too, from those nearing the end of life's journey, who, through the nepenthe of increasing years felt a throb of pain for the man so sorely stricken; and there were letters from children who knew not what lasting grief was, but who, when they heard that the doctor with the kindly face had bowed his whitened head and wept bitterly over the loss of the strong, helpful son and his bright, beloved daughter, took up their pens and wrote to him in their unformed, informal style. All these letters tell of the deep hold he had on the affections of his fellow-beings, how his own lovableness brought their sympathy to be balm to his wounds.

have been rendered painless, and which has in many cases made that possible which would otherwise have been too hazardous to attempt, deserve some special recognition from the Crown.

The Queen has been pleased to command me to offer you on these grounds the rank of Baronet.

I trust it will be agreeable to you to accept the honour.

I remain, yours very truly,

RUSSELL.

CHAPTER X

MORE WORK—THE PRINCIPALSHIP—FAILING

> 'New occasions teach new duties,
>   Time makes ancient things uncouth;
> They must upward still and onward,
>   Who would keep abreast of truth.'
>
> RUSSELL LOWELL.

KEEPING up a warfare on behalf of Acupressure employed him during the first half of the sixties, but, as usual, he had many other irons in the fire, which, by his persistent thrift of time, he was able to heat red-hot. Archæology was his holiday task. Fife caves, cup-marked stones, and ancient sculptures, a discussion over the Pyramids,—all had his attention. He rode other hobbies as well as his antiquarian ones. He was full of schemes for the comfort and befriending of the students of his Alma Mater, whose loneliness in the grey stony centre of Modern Athens he knew so well. He originated the idea and helped to start a restaurant for students within the walls of the University.

Once, when a ball was arranged to welcome home one of his elder boys, he invited his class, on the day of the dance, to the festivity. His invitation was received with cordial cheers. His home circle, with an irate

Jarvis at their head, were flabbergasted when casually, at lunch, he told of the guests he had bidden to the feast. He could not see the difficulties of those in charge of the arrangements. He jumped over them, as was his way. 'If my range of consulting-rooms isn't big enough, send for men and clear out another flat, and get more musicians, and double the order for food supplies. I am sure I always enjoyed a dance when I was their age, and I had to live very simply when I was a student. I will welcome every one of my class, and see they get dancing and supper galore;' and those that came he saw enjoyed themselves.

He occasionally agreed to lecture at various places, mostly on antiquities. He raised a storm at one lecture by advocating the teaching of modern languages *versus* classics. In a letter to one of his sons abroad, he says: 'The longer I have lived, the more I have regretted the state of my knowledge of spoken French, German, etc.; and in all professions the knowledge of languages every day becomes more and more indispensable, because the *new* discoveries, and disquisitions on them, must be read in various languages to enable those running in the race to keep up the required pace.' He knew Latin well himself, so he spoke from his own experience.

He was naturally 'limber-lipped.' He had spoken so well at a British Medical Association meeting in Edinburgh, that it was moved 'that none of them had any idea, with his many eminent acquirements, he possessed in so remarkable a degree the power, of which they that day had a proof, of delivering an address on a difficult subject in the most pleasing and interesting way which one could imagine.' He had fought during its sitting for the Medical Reform Bill, for he had hurried to London, and, as Dr. Christison said: 'In consequence of Dr. Simpson and the friends he had at his command, in the course of one short day —nay, in the course of a very few hours—the alterations were expunged and the Bill restored to its original condition.' The next important work which filled his odd time was the stamping out of smallpox and all infectious diseases. Of a book of his on this subject, numbering six hundred pages, he says: 'It was written at desultory and disconnected intervals, generally amid the incessant calls and toils of practice, and sometimes when, by sickness and fatigue, I was incapacitated from any professional work.' He foresaw future generations would laugh at our blind ignorance in letting preventible diseases live cheek by jowl with us. A great advance towards their removal has been made since he first took the matter in hand. About 1868, one of his resident assistants, Dr. Aitken, took scarlet fever in Queen Street. He was relegated to a top flat, and orders given for his isolation; but Jarvis, who had an old-fashioned dislike to nurses, attended the sick doctor himself, and continued his work downstairs. We from the schoolroom liked the victim who was isolated, and, against orders, paid him visits, and learned our lessons in his room. We had taken all the usual infectious diseases, measles, chickenpox, and scarlet fever, in gangs together, for once one got it in those days, it was the fashion for the others to follow suit at the same time, by herding together. I suppose nowadays no day-school would receive a pupil who came from a house where an infectious case was laid up, but such a thing then was not dreamed of, though my father, by suggesting that this mode of stamping out such complaints should form part of every nursery education, was held as Quixotic. He thought inoculation would eradicate other diseases besides smallpox. He was always trying something new, always full of schemes of philanthropy, and applying discoveries in science to purposes of practical utility. Long before the days when 'slumming' became fashionable, he showed many in the New Town how the inhabitants in the Old Town lived. He constantly made up parties, and went of an evening through the wynds and purlieus of Old Edinburgh, when the overcrowded hive of its inhabitants was astir. I was taken one night with the slummers, and remember how the detectives were congratulated by the people, who all knew my father, for once in a while being in respectable company. 'Is that yoursel', Sir James?' 'Glad to see you, Doctor,' met us as we went through the throng, and many a grimy hand was held out in welcome. Finally, the 'Punch and Judy' man, returned from Musselburgh races, and lodging not far from where Burke and Hare had carried on their nefarious trade, gave us a performance. The guest they all hailed as a well-known friend was deeply interested at the length one mountebank would insert a sword into his throat.

Versifying had been a relaxation of my father's in his student days, and throughout his career he often broke out into 'doggerel fun.' It was one of the double lines of rail he had, whereby he could compass so much work. Archæology was the big double line which relieved the pressure caused by toiling on one highway, and kept, so to speak, the permanent way clear during years of unresting labour. He wrote many verses in albums. 'The Shipwrecked Crew,' 'My Fatherland,' 'To a Pansy,' were some pieces long hoarded in old-world scrap-books. He also wrote some verses on 'A Nightingale in Kinneil Woods,' whither one of these charming minstrels of the night had strayed. In regard to the subject of this last poem, Sir James used to tell how the Linlithgowshire villagers turned out to hear this southern singer, and a Bathgate weaver, after listening to its warble, remarked, with a contemptuous voice, 'It's naething mair than a yellow yoit gane gyte.' Sir James scribbled on his card a rhyming excuse for absence which still exists—

>   Dr. S., with great regret,
>   Finds himself so much beset
>   With sickly, dead and dying,
>   As almost sets his eyes a-crying;
>   Hence, ye of 23,
>   Pray don't wait for him to tea.

And in the press of work those odds and ends of rhymes he scattered about amused him and sent him about his business with a twinkle in his eye. He found that 'a merry heart goes all the day.' He sent back a chicken's breast bone he had got at supper to his hostess, with some lines, entitled 'Sleepy Snatches from my Rhyming Dream, and Ruminations regarding my excellent Chicken, accompanied by the worthy creature's breast bone.' Ever and anon he was seized with what he called the 'rhyming fit,' and some of his best verses he wrote when scampering abroad in 1867, and sent them to his sister-in-law, Miss Grindlay. 'I have often,' he wrote along with them, 'had your song, "Oft in the stilly night," running in my head of late, and got a cup of green tea from Mrs. Lombard, which kept me awake. Their only merit is, they were written at the Lake of Geneva, which is so full of fond recollections to every leal Scotsman.' The words have a pathetically tired ring in them, as if this 'world-weary flesh' of his were longing for 'sleep after toil; port after stormy seas,' and were full of ultimate assurance and trust of a final Home of Rest.

> Oft midst this world's ceaseless strife,
>   When flesh and spirit fail me,
> I stop and think of another life
>   Where ills will ne'er assail me;
> Where my wearied arm shall cease its fight,
>   My heart shall cease its sorrow,
> And this dark night changed for the light
>   Of an everlasting morrow.
>
> On earth below there's naught but woe,
>   E'en mirth is gilded sadness;
> But in heaven above there's nought but love
>   And all its raptured gladness;
> There till I come waits me a home,
>   All human dreams excelling,
> In which at last, when life is past,
>   I'll find a regal dwelling.
>
> Then shall be mine, through grace divine,
>   A rest that knows no ending,
> Which my soul's eye would fain descry,
>   Though still with clay 'tis blending;
> And, Saviour dear, while I tarry here,
>   Where a Father's love has found me,
> O let me feel, through woe and weal,
>   Thy guardian arm around me.

The American War in the 'sixties' had been a source of much excitement to him. He had patients and pupils in both North and South, and many an animated discussion arose among Americans from both sides, who met in his memorable dining-room. The newspapers were taken to him the moment they arrived, as from seven to eight A.M. was his only chance of studying the history of our own times. Well versed he was in the news of the day. Jarvis had the deliverers of the *Scotsman*, *Courant*, and *Daily Review* well trained, by bribery or fear, to come at sharp seven. When his master came down to read prayers at 8.15, he used to drop the papers over the banisters, leaving his hands free to carry other books. The unfolded papers floating down was a sign he was coming, as he usually started them a few minutes previous to his own descent. He was never an active politician, except when, as in 1858, politics touched on medical reform, or when he canvassed for and supported, in his own county of Linlithgowshire, his friend Sir John Pender, of Atlantic Cable fame. Sir James was a Liberal, but in politics, as in religion, he was open-minded and not given to bigotry. He welcomed the pioneers of the lady doctors, when others looked on them with scorn. He liked to give everyone and everything a fair trial. To enumerate all the various works he engaged in or set agoing outside his practice would take as many pages as would the honours which he received. When his book on *Archaic Sculptures* was published, a reviewer, speaking of it, says: 'That the most accomplished, most distinguished of our physicians should consentaneously be one of the most distinguished of Scottish archæologists, does not surprise us. Whatever Sir James sets his mind on, he makes it completely his own—only to make it over to humanity. The last of these transfers is before us in this singularly beautiful quarto, which would have delighted Monkbarns by its contents, and fascinated Miss Wardour by its appearance. What will the great pain-destroyer give us next? An epic poem, a treatise on the calculus, or a grammar of the Pictish language? None of them would take us by surprise.' His medical fame, and consequently his practice, had been growing yearly, till its proportions were such as have never been surpassed by any other medical man. Then, also, so many sought after him, wanting his advice on matters outside medicine. His advice and sympathy in everything came from the heart, therefore went to the heart. He had the subtle quality of understanding people, and, with a wealth of goodwill, was aye ready to respond to them.

Some patient gave him a photograph album full of men he had known, which I now own. Those in it who were photographed as young promising dandies are now grey-haired leaders of men. Others were frail and far advanced in years, and have so long since left this world, that already they seem to belong to another age. It begins with the royal family, when some of them were still small boys dressed in the kilt. The Professor, writing from London about 1850, sent messages to two lads of his own in blouses: 'We saw the spot where King Charles was beheaded. I have been an hour in the British Museum, revelling in some Roman antiquities. I saw Prince Albert yesterday; very kind and gentlemanly; showed me his library, etc.; talked of *Punch*, Scotland, and chloroform. I went over the Palace, and was introduced to the Prince of Wales, Prince Alfred, and the two youngest children.' The photographs range through the nobility, premiers, judges, the African explorers, the Church of England bishops and archbishops, poetry, literature, art, and actors. I doubt if my father was ever in a theatre, but any member of the theatrical profession who was in need of medical advice in Edinburgh received a welcome at No. 52. Among the ladies in this album, though women in his day did not take so prominent a public place as now, are Florence Nightingale, Mrs. Gaskell, Mrs. Norton, Sarah Tytler, Mrs. Oliphant, Mrs. Kean, Mrs. Scott Siddons, Miss Cushman, and Miss Helen Faucit. The latter sent him a pass for a box one evening when she acted 'King Réné's Daughter.' We went as his representatives, and the first play one sees is never forgotten.

In 1868, Sir David Brewster (whose portrait is in this album) died. Sir James and he were old friends. He mentions in a letter of 1860 : 'Yesterday we had twenty-eight at dinner here, meeting Sir David and Lady Brewster, our new Principal. They are living in my cottage at Trinity for a month or two, as they could not get a house in town.' The Council of the Royal Society asked Sir James to move a resolution of admiration for the genius, and regret at the loss of this 'arch-priest of science.' Sir James did so, and ended his eloquent speech in the following words : 'His self-imposed task only ended with his life. And on the subject, it seems to me, I carry almost a mission from him to us—from the dead to the living; for when I last visited him at Allerly, he was within a few hours of death.' Besides his work as a philosopher, Sir James spoke of the Principal as one who formed a link with a brilliant past, and had been a member of 'the constellation of friends that had clustered round the great Wizard of the North at Abbotsford.' He reviewed Sir David's life's work, and went on to picture, touchingly and tenderly, the old man's last days of work, his pleading to return to his study for the last time, till his 'spirit even now seems to me to be beckoning on the votaries of literature and science, here and elsewhere, along that path which he has so gloriously trod, upwards, and heavenwards, and Christwards.'

Sir David Brewster's death left the Principalship of Edinburgh University vacant. In a letter to an old assistant, 6th April 1868, he says: 'The public—not myself—have set me forward as a candidate for the Principalship; but I have not yet applied. I believe it lies between me and Sir A. Grant of Bombay. The time of election is not fixed, *and I will not be greatly disappointed if it does not fall on me.*' Remarkable unanimity among the people of Scotland prevailed in favour of Sir James. He was patriotic. He had refused to leave his country for London, though, had he consented, 'an income unequalled in the history of medical practice awaited him.' When Edinburgh University was mentioned abroad, he was always associated with it as its most brilliant ornament. 'You come from Scotland?' said the King of Denmark to a Scot presented to him. 'Yes, sire, from Edinburgh.' 'From Edinburgh?' replied the king. 'Sir Simpson was of Edinburgh;' and many all over the world besides this king, connected Scotland's capital and Simpson together; for as the Lord Provost said of him, he was 'as well known on the banks of the Thames and the Seine as on the shores of the Firth of Forth.' Foreign countries had showered their honours on him till their list swelled into pages; but after his name he usually wrote only M.D. and the D.C.L. degree he got from Oxford in 1866.

His hospitality, as we have seen, was boundless. As an eminent Edinburgh doctor lately said: 'Anyone had but to tell him of a foreigner or a stranger of distinction being in Edinburgh, and he asked all the men he thought they would like to meet to dinner, and entertained them royally on a moment's notice.' 'Since the days of Sir Walter Scott, we doubt,' said the *Lancet* of him, 'if there was a Scotsman who commanded so much hearty and loyal affection from all grades of the people. He typified in his own person so much in which the Scottish nation prides itself. He was a son of the soil; he was the architect of his own fortunes; he was pious without cant, God-fearing without austerity. His house was a sort of metropolitan Abbotsford in the easy access enjoyed by the stranger, from whatever part of the world he came, with or without a formal introduction.'

Dr. Duns, in his Memoir of Sir James, said: 'As regards literary and scientific accomplishments, it may be said, without fear of contradiction, that there was no other Scotsman who at the time took hold of and influenced more men of mark in every rank and profession than he did.' With such a record, it might be thought he would have easily won the Principalship, but he was not elected. Old partisan feeling, which had smouldered since he had gained his chair, burst anew into flame. It had been fed by his many fights, for his blows were heavy and irresistible; and even when in the wrong, his force of intellect and his ingenuity often cornered his antagonist. He excelled in controversy, and because he was so formidable an opponent, his enemies were full of envy, fear, and ofttimes spleen. The influence he had exercised during the canvassing for various vacant chairs added the losing candidates to the roll against him; also jealousy in some, chagrin at non-success in others, made many of them vindictive against the popular, prosperous man of genius. They consolidated into the strength of union, and threatened, in a memorial to the curators, a species of strike of twelve of the Professors, adding that Sir James's election would bring no ultimate good to the University. 'I have lost the Principalship,' he said quietly to his guests at breakfast, having read before prayers a letter saying a timid curator had withdrawn his support. A counter-memorial was presented in a few days, and signed by nearly a thousand members of the University Council, showing how strong the convictions of educated men were in his favour. His enemies assailed his character in a despicable way. He tried to postpone the election till he vindicated himself, but his enemies or the Senatus hurried matters on. The libellous letter, however, a committee of Sir James's friends traced to its source, and made the circulators thereof retract, and abjectly apologise for its contents. He felt the attacks made on him deeply. Dr. Duns mentions 'the unspeakable sadness' of his face when he heard of the underhand doings of his enemies. They wounded him truly to the heart—a heart always willing to forgive, but which had not the strength to fight against injustice and slanders as in the days of old.

In 1868 he gave the graduation address to the students. It was a brilliant one, for in it he prophesied of the advancement of medicine very accurately. Twenty-five years later, a London daily paper had a leader on this marvellous foresight of his as to the future. He was a fluent speaker, and his voice fell pleasantly on the ear. He was never embarrassed if called upon for an impromptu address, but with that persistent painstaking which led him on to success, when he knew he had a speech to make, he prepared it beforehand. A lady told me she and her mother were having four o'clock tea with him, when he started up, seized some papers, beckoned to her, and with his rapid 'Come away now,' drove off to the Tolbooth Church where the Established Church holds its Assembly. Not explaining his intention, he sent her to the back of the gallery with a roll of papers, while he stood at the desk, and adjured her to 'follow me in print, and if I make a mistake, haul me up, and stop me whenever you don't hear me distinctly;' and he rehearsed without a fault this last graduation address he was to deliver. 'I hate a sermon which is read,' he said, when done, 'so I committed that speech to memory. Come away back to 52, and we'll tell them we've been to church.' In 1868, also, he received the Freedom of the City of Edinburgh from his friend, Lord Provost Dr. William Chambers, and answered the address in an able impromptu speech, in which he reviewed his Edinburgh life from the time he had entered its University, full forty years before.

The old Infirmary had been condemned; the present one, on an airier site and newer principles, was being spoken of, when Sir James, not content with having ameliorated pain within its walls, had long been studying how to reduce its death-rate. He made a stout attempt to introduce a system of cottage hospitals. Within a stone building with its immovable woodwork the death-rate increases yearly. The walls and woodwork become impregnated with a foulness which increases disease. Disinfectants, antiseptics, and newer sanitary improvements have made a stride towards combating this evil; but Sir James, by a thorough series of statistics, proved that operations performed in cottages, with all the faults of ignorance as regards food and nursing against them, had fewer fatal cases than in a hospital with the best nourishment and tending.

'In recording our opinion of Simpson as a professional man, there are four great subjects with which his name will be identified,' said a paper. 'These are the introduction of chloroform, the stamping out of zymotic disease, the introduction of acupressure, and hospital reform.'

His crusade against stone hospitals was not fought out. He issued pamphlets, and was in the thick of battle; but before he annihilated these sources of death, he had to cease his fight; he had to lay down his weapons. As in a posthumous poem called *Prometheus* addressed to him, the writer said—

> 'Shall we a harder doom rehearse?
> . . . .
> Mangled and writhing limbs he lulled to rest,
> And stingless left the old Semitic curse.
> Him, too, for these blest gifts did Zeus amerce?
> He, too, had vultures tearing at his breast.'

His heart, always on the alert to save others, was overstrained, and he was soon to fall a victim to angina pectoris. He had taken a few years before for his motto, '*Victo Dolore*,' but only in 'the peace profound,' as far as he personally was concerned, was he victorious over pain. In his last months on earth he only conquered by enduring what he could not abolish. Very bravely did he face the suffering which beset him when launched on that great river whose sea is death; but he knew that 'death is the quiet haven for us all.'

CHAPTER XI

OVERWORK TELLS—HIS END

> 'A nobler spirit never fled
> From earth. To know him was to love him.
>
> . . . . . .
>
> No sculptured stone need carve his fame
> Telling his short impressive story,
> From heart to lip springs Simpson's name,
> Whene'er we speak of Scotland's glory.'
>
> *Poem on J. Y. S. by T. M'K.*

SIR JAMES had inherited from his ancestors a good constitution. His grandfather, Alexander Simpson, like many who had to be out in 'foul or fair,' tilling his few acres, had suffered from rheumatism, as well as his father before him. Sir James's mother died at forty-nine. Except in her case the Jervays were a long-lived race. On their tombstone in the old kirkyard close to their farm of Boghall, this record of them for a century bears witness they were laid to rest well up in years, and they, along with the Simpsons of Slackend, mostly saw over fourscore and ten. If their distinguished descendant, who maybe from their long-fallow brains reaped his harvest of genius, had lived with more self care for his health and less suicidal energy, with his broad frame and sound constitution he might have survived his contemporaries. 'What vast work for the instruction and benefit of humanity in endless directions would have been done by him, had it pleased Providence to continue his life in this world! Considering what he did, it is impossible to hint what he might have done in say twenty years, with his powers at their ripest,' wrote an advocate lately to me. If he had had leisure even for travel, he would have found much to instruct him, and much to improve others. America he wanted to see, and the 'gorgeous East,' and Egypt with its ancient remains.

Very early in his career there crop up little notices of ill health, brought on, he confesses, by overstrain or worry. From time to time, but unwillingly, he had to give in and take a day or two in the house. When thus forced to lay down the lancet, he took up his other weapon, the pen, believing 'the labour we delight in physics pain.' Numberless well-wishers, when he was still young in years, though already old in experience, appealed to him for the benefit of others to be less unselfish, and warned him of the certain results of his reckless overwork. 'Take care of yourself, dearest friend, for the sake of science and mankind,' wrote a distinguished doctor to him. After his eldest son's death, brief notices in his letters tell of frequent suffering. His very scampers wearied him. 'I must be greatly stronger before I can work again,' he wrote in 1866. When laid up with sciatica in Mona's Isle, he says: 'I have walked several times in pure *despite*, and I think it is yielding.' He was vexed to think pain had made him a tiresome visitor, and wrote to his niece on his return: 'I often feel ashamed of all the trouble which I, in my petulance and sickness, caused you, and though we may never meet on earth again, believe me, my dear Maggie, I shall never forget your goodness to me.'

In 1867 he was off his class work the first part of the winter session, and his prolonged illness gave rise to many reports of Saughton or Morningside being his destination. Jarvis told him of these statements, and thought he was fitting himself for their realisation by 'no' resting, seeing folk, ill as he is, and writing a book.' He had trained himself from his college days to do with a short shrift of sleep, but a blink of rest was to him 'a sweet enjoyment,' a rarity worthy to chronicle in his letters: 'Such a sleep last night—a whole eight hours' sleep, and no bell. I feel quite fresh,' were put into notes written to those away. 'You must be very tired, Doctor, sitting up all night,' a mother of a patient said to him. 'Not a bit,' he said. 'There was a bairn's bed in the corner of the room, and I curled myself up like a dog, and had a nap.'

Viewbank he fled to sometimes to enjoy the luxury of a real good sleep. When it was let one winter, he drove down to his mother-in-law's, whose house was near by his own at Trinity. He arrived after his lecture. 'My e'en are gone thegither with sleep,' he said, and told how warily he had escaped from his home and patients, sent his carriage back from the Waverley Station with word he would not return till ten at night, then hired a cab. 'Waken me at nine, and give me tea and an egg, and hide my hat, it is such a tell-tale,' he said. He then rolled into a feather bed and was asleep before his hostess had well realised he had arrived. He was unwillingly wakened when his cab returned at 9.30, and devoutly hoped he would be allowed another eight hours' sleep at 52, to 'set him up.' Before leaving he glanced round the room, which was full of the Liverpool furniture among which he had first seen his wife, his eye melting in tenderness as it lit on one of Jamie's last pieces of carpentry, on a mussel shell, on a bit of marble his Sunbeam had bought out of her very own purse when away on a scamper with him; and there, below the Chippendale sideboard that had been purchased by Mrs. Grindlay at Bo'ness on her marriage in 1796, lay a furred foot-warmer which 'Dr. David's' first fee had bought. 'How proud he and his mother were of it!' said his father, as he said good-bye to 'the grandmother of ninety years.'

Railway journeys in Sir James's time were not so luxurious as now. A Pullman would have been a godsend to him. He would have then looked forward to a night journey to London as one of secured, undisturbed sleep. The very arms of the first-class carriages a quarter of a century ago were immovable. To try to gain ease, he had a simple invention of his own, consisting of three sticks joined by cloth hinges, which he put across from seat to seat, and borrowed an extra cushion if he had a carriage to himself. He considered this a good approach to a comfortable bed. He had a lamp, too, with sharp claws to fasten on the braid of the cushion, to enable him to read, if sleep were denied him. He could always solace himself with his books, a good bagful of which he carried with him, but these uncomfortable carriages made his endless journeys very exhausting. He suffered from the cold and draughts. 'You've left your three new flannel shirts behind you, sir,' Jarvis reported reproachfully, when he had sought in vain for them in his master's bag. 'No, I brought them with me,' said his master, with a gleam of fun lighting up his tired face as he safely contradicted his positive servant. 'I have got them *all* on. I wished last night I had three more, and I wish now I could get five minutes' privacy to take them all off.'

He never met with any railway accident, constantly as he journeyed, except once, when the bottom of the carriage in which he was sitting was splintered. But he coiled himself and his books up on the seat till the express's next stop. He was often storm-stayed, and had weary waits at stations, where the officials, high and low, welcomed him; the engine-drivers invited him to their fire and brewed tea for him, if the waiting-rooms were shut. Much railway information he would bring home, for he never lost an opportunity of finding how his fellow-beings fared. Continually he would desire a knitted waistcoat, or a keepsake of some kind, to be sent to some kindly guard who specially befriended him, some wayside stationmaster who had fed and fired him when hungry and cold.

One bitter winter's morning, someone recalled lately how, when snow blocked the way, the train came to a standstill, and while all the passengers, chilled, cross, and hungry, fumed, Sir James, in a long sealskin surtout a grateful patient had given him, walked up and down to warm himself, for, notwithstanding all his furs, he was cold. He found a third-class carriage of shivering, starved children, crying with misery. He got the stationmaster coaxed into making some tea, piled his rug and newspapers upon the little ones, incited others to help, inspired all into more hopeful views of life, till the fire of his presence thawed them into geniality, and when the delayed train reached Edinburgh, it was commented on as being the first which had arrived that day not filled with enraged and grumbling passengers. 'It's all that man,' said the guard, pointing to Sir James, who was hurrying off. 'It's a mercy we a' like him, and coont it a pleasure to aye find his belongings, or he'd never own a rug or portmanteau.'

But kindly attentions not often bestowed on other travellers, coffee wired ahead for him, bidden to fires from which others were debarred, would not save him from hardships. He had startled the patients waiting to see him by the shrill cry of pain wrung from him when his willing heart at last rebelled at overwork. He could not do without sleep for nights on end, as heretofore, but still he struggled on. Early in 1870 he had some fatal journeys. He had to give his opinion in a legal case in London. His evidence was delayed, but the telegram came too late to save him the journey. Twice in a week, in bitter weather, he travelled up and down to London, and that, beside other night journeys which kept him out of bed, practically gave him his death. His opinion on the Mordaunt case, time has proved to be correct. A paper, speaking of this trial, said: 'It will not be forgotten how his personal influence and manner held the Court as it were enthralled, while he gave unchecked, as on ordinary occasions, a lengthy exposition, almost amounting to a clinical lecture, on the case.' The second time he arrived in London that fatal week, he went to his old pupil Sir William Priestley's house. His host was shocked to see him. He was suffering so intensely from cold that he could hardly shave himself.

He was shaken by constant travel, blue, and frozen to the marrow. After giving his evidence, he stopped at York on his homeward journey, dined at Lord Houghton's, and went to chat with a medical friend till the night mail picked him up. He 'rested' the remainder of that journey on the floor of the carriage, pain from sciatica and heart exhaustion not allowing him to obtain ease otherwise. A few days later, he took the last of his countless professional journeys to Perth, lectured to his students, came home completely prostrate, and took to his room. This was in February 1870. In March, writing to his youngest son, but recently gone abroad, he reported, 'I am not able to exert my pen'; but speaks hopefully of going to Spain, and told how he was reading all in connection with this hoped-for trip. It was suggested that this, the youngest of his boys, should return home. But seeing how his sufferings wrung the hearts of his nurses (his wife, his son, his assistant, and Jarvis nursed him, for sick-nurses then did not take possession of every sick-room), he resolved to leave the young student at Geneva. He warned him, however, 'At times I feel very, very ill indeed, as if I should be soon called away'; and he wrote in a postscript to this letter: 'Let me add how happy you have ever made me, how dearly and deeply I love you.' Many times that March, in the night, those who watched him, and the doctors who were ever at his side, feared he would never see another daybreak. In his frequent brief attacks of illness, when sciatica chained him to his bed, his books would collect in his room. He used to complain in his bachelor days that his sofa was so fond of books, he never got a rest on it, for its desire to be learned kept it piled deep in literature. During this last illness it seemed as if his library would gradually move upstairs. He revised his archæological works, wrote more, and saw patients,—some even were carried up to his room. To save others the long stairs he had so often panted up, he was moved to the drawing-room, which became that wonderful sick-room where, as he had said of Sir David Brewster, 'Faith made to him the dreaded darkness of the valley of death a serene scene of beauty and brightness.' It was a room little associated with him except on Sundays, which he liked to spend quietly, and give the door bell and his servants a chance of a holiday. When he was forced to take a 'half rest,' he hid in the drawing-room for a day, as being more private than that hospitable dining-room, through whose door all Edinburgh claimed a right to walk. He was wheeled into the outer room during the day. No amount of suffering dulled his keen interest in all that was going on around, even to most trivial details. He helped me daily with my lessons, and had always a list of books at his tongue's end which would bear on my school work. He had had but little time to loiter in his own family circle, but he condensed into a few moments, as was his way, a world of interest and love. He would suddenly ask what work was being prepared in the schoolroom, and tell where references in regard to subjects could be got, or recite some historic tale which would fix a date in a slippery memory. Our object was usually to scamper through our lessons in a superficial way, as long as we were not kept in. He overwhelmed us with suggestions for hunting out the most distant facts in connection with any prescribed task. He would hint to us where to find some apt quotation which would give a finish to an essay, and the trouble he took, when our lessons diverted his attention, to seek for such shamed the idlest of us into looking up the references for ourselves. During his illness I every day learned my lessons in his sick-room. He took a keen interest in them, and was eager to know if his suggestions had won commendation in the day's task. He enjoyed a chat with friends, and if breathlessness hampered his speech, he, with a brave smile, begged the other to 'Talk away, it cheers me up.' Robert Simpson, his nephew (his brother Sandy's 'Benjamin'), came in one day to tell him, with regard to his own prospects (about which his uncle was concerned), that through his interest in philanthropic work he had received the offer of a partnership in an old-established legal business. His uncle was radiant with delight. He told everyone like an eager child what was to him good news, and pictured Sandy's pleasure that his son's career was assured. 'Tell me, what are you going to speak to your Brigade boys on to-night?' he would ask Robert, and would thereupon give hints to illustrate the text chosen. He never failed to question my cousin if those hints had told well.

He set himself to realise what of this world's gear he had to leave behind him. He gave this young nephew and lawyer charge of all his legal affairs. He faced all difficulties in regard to them. He never for a moment regretted his lavish open-handedness, his prodigal generosity in attending so many without remuneration. His only sigh was given when he wished he had been busier, and had had more time to give to studying, so as more effectually to eradicate disease. With loving forethought for me, his youngest and only remaining daughter, he mapped out my remaining school years and line of study. Also, from among all his thousand and one women friends, after thinking long, with that divining mind of his, he bade his nephew write to one whose fidelity he wisely trusted. He asked her to be, not a legal guardian full of red tape authority, but a guardianess who would give of her womanly love and liberal heart to one who with prophetic prevision he foresaw would soon be doubly orphaned. He thus provided me with a friend indeed. When he had made a review of his worldly affairs for the benefit of those who came after him, he troubled no more on the subject.

Hopefully, patiently, he waited for the end. Death had no terrors for him; 'a rest that knows no ending' was to my father a blessed outlook. 'Ease after war doth greatly please,' he could truly say. He liked having Robert with him, and again and again thanked him for spending his spare hours by his side. He could not, with that humility ever characteristic of him, realise that he was conferring a benefit. 'Stay to-night,' he would plead. 'I would like you to be here, and I may slip away any moment.'

This nephew kept a journal in which he daily jotted down his uncle's views and sayings, and in it Sir James's unselfish spirit conspicuously appears. His thoughts and his talk were always of others. Even invalidism could not make him self-centred. He liked being read aloud to. His wife had a pleasing, soft voice, and she read *Orfie Sibbald, Oliver Underwood, Teddie's First and Last Sacrament*—simple tales he took a pleasure in. Any book he fancied, with that love of giving and sharing that was so strong within him, he ordered copies of to be sent to friends. 'In Immanuel's Land' was a hymn which was one of his chief favourites. He knew the author[1] and had long been familiar with her noble works, as well as with Samuel Rutherford's last words from 'fair Anwoth.' When his 'sands of time' were sinking, he asked the hymn to be read and re-read to him. His nephew knew his favourite psalms and chapters, and would repeat them to him in the sleepless nights, when the watchers yearned for the day to break. 'Stop a moment, say that again,' his uncle would often say, as texts came to him with a new meaning, for as the light of this life faded from him, 'stars invisible by day' shone and lit up the coming darkness of the valley of shadow.

As the days lengthened into April, he had to give up sleeping in the inner drawing-room, and spend the night propped erect by pillows in the airier, larger room. He rallied again, and I was sent off to the Highlands for the spring vacation. He deemed a house under the pall of sickness was not holiday ground, and knew that, with the easy-mindedness of youth I would fear no immediate ill. When I went to say good-bye on the morning I left, he turned to me, saying 'My daughter, oh, my daughter!' quoting the words he had used to greet his first-born. He said them with such a peculiarly sad thrill in his

---

[1] She wrote a poem on his death, from which one verse may not be amiss here—

'No rest for him in heart or hand or brain ;
No pause the o'er wearied frame, work to attune ;
No truce in the stern war with human pain,
Till sudden sleep closed life's bright afternoon.'

voice, which was always tenderly soft, that they smote on my careless ears. Seeing I was struck by his tones, he kissed me and cheerily bade me go and enjoy myself, and with another sigh of 'My daughter, oh, my daughter!' waved me off, but watched me leave him with a yearning, melting fondness in his eyes. When I saw him two weeks later, the anæsthesia of nature had come to bury his pain in oblivion. To ease his labouring breath, someone sat by his pillow. On his last night on earth, my uncle begged for this post, and my father laid his head on his brother's knee, murmuring often 'Sandy, Sandy'; whether he knew him, or whether his mind had wandered off to the days when he had sat on that brother's knee, a laughing lad, we knew not. Just as the sun was setting, on the 6th of May 1870, his life's journey came to its close, and the ceaseless toil of his well-filled fifty-eight years was over. With a soft sigh as of infinite relief, he passed 'To where beyond these voices there is peace.'

For his body a resting-place was offered in Westminster Abbey,—an honour seldom bestowed on one of his profession,—but his wife preferred that he should be laid to rest in Scottish soil, in the city he had so dearly loved, and which he had chosen as the field of his labours. His helpmate for thirty years, when she decided against the far-off solitariness of Westminster, felt they would not long be separated. Before the daisies had reared their heads on the turf over him, my mother was laid beside him. Warriston, he had often spoken of as his final resting-place, looking up to the grey-towered city, with its background of green hills. 'I have bought a piece of ground in the new cemetery for mine and me,' he wrote when his eldest child died. He had since then laid four other children there beside her.

Edinburgh accorded the man who had first entered her gates a footsore boy in his teens, a funeral such as she had never given to another citizen. Business was suspended, and on the 13th of May, in the city he had worked in, 'one street alone was crowded—it led but to the tomb.' The spectators went not from curiosity to see a stately procession wend past. They, too, went as mourners, not decked with idle 'trappings of woe,' but with sorrow written large on their faces. The hold Sir James had on the hearts of his fellow-beings was easily seen that day. Scotland sent her noblest and most honoured sons to do him a last honour, and the inhabitants of Edinburgh's closes and wynds helped to line the way. Newhaven men and women in their fishing garb stood weeping in the throng. The stern reticence of the Scotch, a nation not given to wearing their hearts upon their sleeves, was melted into tears as the multitude on that May day silently watched the bier pass to its chosen resting-place. To those mourners he was not only the world-renowned doctor, but to each personally their 'beloved physician,' their trusted friend and benefactor.

He had often stood by the burial-place of the Jervays of Boghall, in the old kirkyard at Bathgate, and traced there, on their weather-worn headstone, the hour-glass which surmounted it. But to him the hour-glass spoke of only 'the sands of time.' He looked ever forward to the time when 'the dawn of heaven would break.' In the centre of the ground he acquired at Warriston, when first the 'dews of sorrow' gathered on his young brow, he placed an obelisk, pointing, like the church spires, heavenward. On it he carved 'Nevertheless I live,' and above it a butterfly. So there he rests, with the emblem of immortality soaring above him!

www.ingramcontent.com/pod-product-compliance
Lightning Source LLC
Chambersburg PA
CBHW030315170426
43202CB00009B/1014